OTHER PUBLICATIONS FROM THE DRUCKER FOUNDATION

Organizational Leadership Resource
The Drucker Foundation Self-Assessment Tool

The Drucker Foundation Future Series
The Leader of the Future, *Frances Hesselbein, Marshall Goldsmith, Richard Beckhard, Editors*
The Organization of the Future, *Frances Hesselbein, Marshall Goldsmith, Richard Beckhard, Editors*
The Community of the Future, *Frances Hesselbein, Marshall Goldsmith, Richard Beckhard, Richard F. Schubert, Editors*

Wisdom to Action Series
Leading for Innovation, *Frances Hesselbein, Marshall Goldsmith, Iain Somerville, Editors*
Leading Beyond the Walls, *Frances Hesselbein, Marshall Goldsmith, Iain Somerville, Editors*

Leaderbooks
The Collaboration Challenge: How Nonprofits and Businesses Succeed Through Strategic Alliances, *James E. Austin*
Meeting the Collaboration Challenge (workbook and video)

Journal and Related Books
Leader to Leader Journal
Leader to Leader: Enduring Insights on Leadership from the Drucker Foundation's Award-Winning Journal, *Frances Hesselbein, Paul Cohen, Editors*
On High-Performance Organizations, *Frances Hesselbein, Rob Johnston, Editors*
On Leading Change, *Frances Hesselbein, Rob Johnston, Editors*
On Mission and Leadership, *Frances Hesselbein, Rob Johnston, Editors*

Video Training Resources
Excellence in Nonprofit Leadership Video, *featuring Peter F. Drucker, Max De Pree, Frances Hesselbein, and Michele Hunt. Moderated by Richard F. Schubert*
Leading in a Time of Change: What It Will Take to Lead Tomorrow, *a conversation with Peter F. Drucker and Peter M. Senge, introduction by Frances Hesselbein*
Lessons in Leadership Video, *with Peter F. Drucker*

Online Resources
www.drucker.org

On Leading Change

A DRUCKER FOUNDATION
LEADERBOOK

ABOUT THE DRUCKER FOUNDATION

The Peter F. Drucker Foundation for Nonprofit Management, founded in 1990, takes its name and inspiration from the acknowledged father of modern management. By providing educational opportunities and resources, the foundation furthers its mission "to lead social sector organizations toward excellence in performance." It pursues this mission through the presentation of conferences, video teleconferences, the annual Peter F. Drucker Award for Nonprofit Innovation, and the annual Frances Hesselbein Community Innovation Fellows Program, as well as through the development of management resources, partnerships, and publications.

The Drucker Foundation believes that a healthy society requires three vital sectors: a public sector of effective governments, a private sector of effective businesses, and a social sector of effective community organizations. The mission of the social sector and its organizations is to change lives. It accomplishes this mission by addressing the needs of the spirit, mind, and body of individuals, the community, and society. This sector and its organizations also create a meaningful sphere of effective and responsible citizenship.

In the ten years after its inception, the Drucker Foundation, among other things:

- Presented the Drucker Innovation Award, which each year generates hundreds of applications from local community enterprises; many applicants work in fields in which results are difficult to achieve

- Worked with social sector leaders through the Frances Hesselbein Community Innovation Fellows program

- Held more than twenty conferences in the United States and in countries around the world

- Developed thirteen books: the *Self-Assessment Tool* (revised 1998), for nonprofit organizations; three books in the Drucker Foundation Future Series, *The Leader of the Future* (1996), *The Organization of the Future* (1997), and *The Community of the Future* (1998); *Leader to Leader* (1999); *Leading Beyond the Walls* (1999); *The Collaboration Challenge* (2000); the *Leading in a Time of Change* viewer's workbook and video (2001); *Leading for Innovation* (2002); and *On Mission and Leadership*, *On Leading Change*, *On High-Performance Organizations*, and *On Creativity, Innovation, and Renewal* (all 2002)

- Developed *Leader to Leader*, a quarterly journal for leaders from all three sectors

- Established a Web site (drucker.org) that shares articles on leadership and management and examples of nonprofit innovation with hundreds of thousands of visitors each year

For more information on the Drucker Foundation, contact:

The Peter F. Drucker Foundation for Nonprofit Management
320 Park Avenue, Third Floor, New York, NY 10022-6839 U.S.A.
Telephone: (212) 224-1174 • Fax: (212) 224-2508
E-mail: info@pfdf.org • Web address: www.drucker.org

On Leading Change

A Leader to Leader Guide

Frances Hesselbein
Rob Johnston
Editors

JOSSEY-BASS
A Wiley Company
www.josseybass.com

Published by

JOSSEY-BASS
A Wiley Company
989 Market Street
San Francisco, CA 94103-1741

www.josseybass.com

Jossey-Bass books and products are available through most bookstores. To contact Jossey-Bass directly, call (888) 378-2537, fax to (800) 605-2665, or visit our Web site at www.josseybass.com.

Substantial discounts on bulk quantities of Jossey-Bass books are available to corporations, professional associations, and other organizations. For details and discount information, contact the special sales department at Jossey-Bass.

We at Jossey-Bass strive to use the most environmentally sensitive paper stocks available to us. Our publications are printed on acid-free recycled stock whenever possible, and our paper always meets or exceeds minimum GPO and EPA requirements.

Library of Congress Cataloging-in-Publication Data

On leading change : a leader to leader guide / Frances Hesselbein and Rob Johnston, editors.
   p. cm.
"Drucker Foundation Leaderbooks."
Includes index.
ISBN 0-7879-6070-5
1. Organizational change. 2. Leadership. I. Hesselbein, Frances. II. Johnston, Rob, date
HD58.8 .O55 2002
658.4'06-dc21   2001007674

FIRST EDITION

HB Printing 10 9 8 7 6 5 4 3 2 1

Contents

Introduction

People in the United States and around the world have an enormous hunger for ideas; that's why in 1996 the Drucker Foundation launched *Leader to Leader*, a journal of ideas by leaders for leaders. This hunger among millions of working executives demonstrates their concern for the future and commitment to making a difference.

The incisive thinkers and remarkable leaders who have contributed to the journal and its related books open doors, spark ideas, raise signal flags, and help satisfy that universal hunger. These extraordinary contributors have taught us, among other things, that great leaders do not live isolated from the world; they are engaged with and deeply care about others. They measure their own success by the real-world impact of their work. That people throughout our society and organizations want to contribute to a better world has been a major premise of *Leader to Leader*.

We learned, too, that astonishing things happen when you give intelligent, effective people a free hand. Never have we approached our authors with an assigned topic or reviewed their work before an advisory board or peer review; when you're working with the best in the world, you don't do that. Rather, we simply asked, "What's on your mind? What issues will most affect leaders, organizations, or communities in the coming years?"

From that unfettered process, several coherent themes emerged with astonishing clarity. They are evident in the four volumes of the Leader to Leader Guides. This volume, *On Leading Change*, explores the challenges of bringing organizations through transformation. Leaders of change encourage the organization to question, innovate, experiment, and learn from mistakes. They prepare for change, seek new perspectives, and broaden participation throughout the organization.

The other volumes in this series are *On Mission and Leadership*, which explores the essential role that mission plays in defining and supporting leadership; *On High-Performance Organizations*, which explores getting the most from the people and other resources of each organization; and *On Creativity, Innovation, and Renewal*, which explores how leaders can keep an organization changing with a focus on building the future.

We gathered the wisdom of our contributors so that our readers could find insight and inspiration to make a difference in their organizations and their communities. We hope our collection will help you to lead, to inspire a change, to strengthen your performance, or to spark and sustain a renewal. We wish you the best as you apply these lessons to the work you do and the people you touch.

February 2002

Frances Hesselbein
Easton, Pennsylvania

Rob Johnston
New York, New York

About the Editors

Frances Hesselbein is chairman of the board of governors of the Peter F. Drucker Foundation for Nonprofit Management and is the former chief executive of the Girl Scouts of the U.S.A. She is a member of the boards of other organizations and corporations and is the lead editor of the Drucker Foundation's bestselling books, including *The Leader of the Future*, *The Organization of the Future*, *The Community of the Future*, *Leading Beyond the Walls*, and *Leader to Leader*, published by Jossey-Bass. She also serves as editor in chief of the journal *Leader to Leader*. She speaks on leadership and management to audiences around the world in the private, nonprofit, and governmental sectors. She has received fifteen honorary doctorates and was awarded the Presidential Medal of Freedom in 1998.

Rob Johnston is president and CEO of the Peter F. Drucker Foundation for Nonprofit Management. He has served the Drucker Foundation since 1991 and was appointed president effective March 2001. At the foundation he has led program development, the Drucker Innovation Award program, publication development, and teleconference and conference development.

He was executive producer for *Leading in a Time of Change*, a 2001 video featuring Peter F. Drucker and Peter M. Senge, and for *The Nonprofit Leader of the Future*, the foundation's 1997 video teleconference broadcast to 10,000 leaders across the United States. He leads the editorial development of the foundation's Web site (drucker.org) and is a senior editor for *Leader to Leader*. Johnston earned a B.A. degree in the history of art from Yale and an M.B.A. degree from Stanford. He contributed a chapter to *Enterprising Nonprofits* (John Wiley & Sons, 2001).

On Leading Change

A DRUCKER FOUNDATION
LEADERBOOK

1

The Key to Cultural Transformation

Frances Hesselbein

*Changing the culture of an organization requires transfor-
mation of the organization's purpose, focus on customers,
and results. Frances Hesselbein explores the seven steps involved: (1) scanning the environment for the few trends
that will have the greatest impact on the organization in the
future; (2) determining the implications of those trends; (3)
re-examining the mission and refining it; (4) dropping the
old hierarchy and creating flexible, fluid management structures and systems that unleash people's energies; (5) challenging assumptions, policies, and procedures and keeping
only those that reflect the desired future; (6) communicating a few compelling messages that mobilize people around
mission, goals, and values; and (7) dispersing the responsibilities of leadership across the organization at every level.*

In times of great change, organizational culture gets special
attention. Leaders issue calls for cultural change, stating:
"We need a more entrepreneurial culture," or, "We must create
a culture of accountability." If we could alter the underlying beliefs of our organizations, the thinking goes, our practices would
surely follow.

But changing the culture of an organization requires a transformation of the organization itself—its purpose, its focus on customers and results. Culture does not change because we desire to change it. Culture changes when the organization is transformed; the culture reflects the realities of people working together every day.

Peel away the shell of an organization and there lives a culture—a set of values, practices, and traditions that define who we are as a group. In great organizations the competence, commitment, innovation, and respect with which people carry out their work are unmistakable to any observer—and a way of living to its members. In lesser organizations, distrust and dysfunction are equally pervasive.

If we note Peter Drucker's definition of innovation—"change that creates a new dimension of performance"—it is the performance that changes the culture—not the reverse.

When I was leading a transformation of one of the largest organizations in the world, with a workforce of over 700,000 adults serving more than 2.2 million young members, our focus was not on changing the culture—though that was a result. Our focus was on building an organization committed to managing for the mission, managing for innovation, and managing for diversity.

Changes in the practices and beliefs of an organization do not happen because someone sits in the executive office and commands them. They happen in the real world, in local communities. The 700,000 women and men who served as volunteers and staff, as well as the parents of the young people served, had to be deeply committed to the goal of equal access and to building a richly diverse organization.

We changed the very face of the organization—the program, the uniforms, the way we trained adults and delivered services, the way we communicated—but never the purpose, the values, the principles, or the promise of a great institution. The changes came through a mission-focused effort that was inclusive and involved those affected by the decisions as well as those implementing them. We listened to our customers—some of them only five years old.

A respected first-time visitor to our headquarters, listening and observing, said, "Rarely have I observed a culture that is so palpable." That culture flowed from the transformation—it changed as the organization changed.

Our passionate purpose was creating opportunities for girls to reach their own highest potential. We concentrated on building a viable, relevant, contemporary organization that truly furthered that purpose. Through that building process, the culture was inexorably changed. The result was the greatest membership diversity in 78 years, coupled with the greatest organizational cohesion anyone could remember. The culture became a powerful reflection of the organization and its people, those who served and those who were served.

From experience and observation, there are seven essential steps to transform a culture through a changed organization:

- *Scanning* the environment for the two or three trends that will have the greatest impact upon the organization in the future
- *Determining* the implications of those trends for the organization
- *Revisiting* the mission—answering Peter Drucker's first classic question, "What is our mission?" and examining our purpose and refining it until it is a short, powerful, compelling statement of why we do what we do

- *Banning* the old hierarchy we all inherited and building flexible, fluid management structures and systems that unleash the energies and spirits of our people

- *Challenging* the gospel of "the way we've always done it" by questioning every policy, practice, procedure, and assumption, abandoning those that have little use today or will in the future—and keeping only those that reflect the desired future

- *Communicating* with the few powerful, compelling messages that mobilize people around mission, goals, and values—not with 50 messages that our people have trouble remembering

- *Dispersing* the responsibilities of leadership across the organization, so that we have not one leader, but many leaders at every level of the enterprise

And along the way, by initiating each of these challenging steps, leaders of the organization, in their behavior and language, embody the mission, values, and principles. By working with others toward change, we create the desired result—the inclusive, cohesive, productive organization reaching new levels of excellence in performance and significance.

Peter Drucker, in *Managing in a Time of Great Change*, makes a powerful statement: "For the organization to perform to a high standard, its members must believe that what it is doing is, in the last analysis, the one contribution to community and society on which all others depend."

That is the marriage of culture and organization, of belief and practice, that marks our best institutions. And in a wonderfully circular way, as the organization and its people grow and flourish, the culture reflects and resounds and delivers a message—changing as the environment and the needs of our customers change.

In the end, it is a good thing that culture is not easily changed. A culture defines the heart of the organization, and a change of heart is not to be taken lightly. But the introspective and inclusive process by which an organization formulates its values and revisits its mission will enable organizations to serve their customers and communities with high performance, to be viable and relevant in an uncertain future. That capacity to change and to serve is the essence of a great and vibrant culture.

Frances Hesselbein is editor in chief of *Leader to Leader,* chairman of the Drucker Foundation, and former chief executive of the Girl Scouts of the USA.

2

Strategies for Change Leaders

A Conversation Between Peter F. Drucker and Peter M. Senge

In late 1999, Peter Drucker and Peter Senge explored some of the challenges of leadership and change. Their conversation touched on many issues, including the pace of change and how leadership can deal with constant change; they discussed the issue of what can be learned from nonprofits. Highlights of their dialogue are presented here.

How can leaders prepare themselves and their organizations for the changes that lie ahead? No question is more fundamental to the success of our business and social institutions. In a remarkable meeting in late 1999, two of the great thinkers of our time—Peter Drucker and Peter Senge—explored the challenges of leadership and change. Their three-hour conversation touched on many issues:

- The discipline of planned abandonment
- The need to focus on opportunities rather than problems
- The importance of preserving institutional values and trust in the midst of change

- What businesses can learn from nonprofits about attracting and mobilizing knowledge workers

Will the pace of change accelerate in the future?

Peter Senge: It's hard to imagine that the next 10 or 20 years are going to bring less change than the past 10 or 20 years. An interesting way to think about this question is to imagine where we were 10 or 20 years ago, and what we would have imagined for the time we've just lived through. What's most useful is not so much predicting specifics, but trying to understand the forces at play. Futurologists love to tell us that we're going to work so many hours, commute so many miles, and so on. But those are just extrapolations, trends. What's extremely difficult in a time like this is to think about what *breaks* the trends.

Peter Drucker: Most people think the last few years have been years of very great change. Actually that's only because the preceding 30 years were so continuous. We are at the point where the transition turns over. We have been through two big transitions in the last 500 years in the West, one starting with Gutenberg and one with the steam engine. After 40 or 50 years there's a total change, and we are just at that point today. One implication is that every organization will have to become a change leader. You can't manage change. You can only be ahead of it. You can only make it.

People say, for instance, that the information revolution is just beginning to have an impact, but nobody predicted the biggest force for change in the information era—e-commerce. E-commerce will make the multinational as we know it today obsolete. At the same time we can say with 90 percent probability that the new industries that are emerging will have nothing to do with information. I will take a risk here and suggest that the most important new industry in the next 30 years will be fish farms. We are moving from being hunters and gatherers on the oceans to being aquaculturalists. There are a few others in the wings, and they have nothing to do with the information technology. They have a lot to do with the new mind-set.

In all probability, the single dominant factor in all developed and emerging countries will be population changes. Only in the English-speaking world, where we accept immigration, will we still have a birthrate barely adequate to maintain the population. In Italy the birth rate is down to about a third of the replacement rate. In Japan it's half the replacement rate. Except in the English-speaking countries, the youth market is over. The extreme youth culture of the last 40 years was based on demographics. It's an old rule that the population group that is both the biggest and growing the fastest determines the mood. Since 1950, in all developed countries, these have been people between 15 and 30, or 12 and 25. Even in the U.S. today, the fastest-growing age group is 55-plus. Nobody quite knows yet what the new mind-set is going to be, because we've never had these demographic changes.

How does an organization and its leadership deal with a world in the vortex of change?

Peter Drucker: First, accept the fact that organizations have to deal with change, and not believe this is something you do on Friday afternoon. Second, leaders have to create receptivity to change, and there is only one way to do it. You have to build organized abandonment into your system. There's nothing that so concentrates a manager's mind as to know that the present product is going to be abandoned in two years. Otherwise you won't innovate, you'll postpone.

Innovation is hard work and you may put in five years before you see any output. In the meantime you are being compensated on this year's results, and you're going to put more money into making the old product, the old service. That's just patching. Every three years, at the least, every organization should sit down and look at every product and every service and say if we didn't do this already, knowing what we now do, would we go do it? If the answer is no, don't make another study, just stop.

Peter Senge: Your notion of planned abandonment raises the question, Why is it so hard for us? Logically it makes a lot of sense. You just can't keep adding in new things. After a while the weight of everything that's there holds you back. A lot of people in the creative arts have a very good feeling for this because you create something and you move on. But once we get into organizations and institutions somehow the dynamics change. As you suggested, it's one thing to say the business is dead and we're losing money like mad, so we must abandon it. But often the right time to abandon is much earlier than that, because trying to maintain this activity is soaking up your creative possibilities.

We do things the way we do because we haven't really thought of other ways to do them. And it is extremely difficult in many organizations to challenge assumptions. It's a career-threatening act for individuals to raise their hand and say wait a second, I have a real question about what we're doing.

Peter Drucker: Once you've gotten over the first couple of years, the process becomes self-supporting, but the start is very difficult. That is because managers, over the course of their career, spend more time with their product or service than with their spouse and children. This is their child, their life. They're emotionally invested. I've seen so many people who have no personality except in their product. But the time to get rid of a product is not when it no longer produces, but when somebody says it still has five good years. That's the time to say cut.

Peter Senge: It seems to me, Peter, we're on to something quite fundamental. There is a difference between *creating* as an orientation toward life and *problem solving*. Our enterprises are so dominated by an ethic of problem solving that it undermines creating—bringing something new into reality. So much of the recognition and rewards system of the organization says, Who fixed what problems? And of course we spend a lot of our time fixing unimportant problems. The real question is, what predominates—creating or problem solving? It seems to me that this basic shift between predominantly creating and predominantly problem solving is profound.

Peter Drucker: You know, I am a little unhappy with all the talk about creativity. To some extent it's a cop-out to cover up our problem focus. There is no lack of creativity. But we are doing our level best in most organizations to squelch it. There are exceptions, quite a few. But by and large, even small businesses find it very hard to experiment. I say to my clients, don't make a study, go out and try it. Where you have a market in which you are strong, and it's sufficiently remote, go test it. In three weeks you'll know 10 times as much as you'll know in any study, at a fraction of the cost.

What else does it take for an organization to lead change?

Peter Drucker: You have to infuse your entire organization with the mind-set that change is an opportunity and not a threat. That takes hard work. And then you have to work with two hands. One is the systematic right hand where you methodically look at changes. You start out looking for unexpected success, because that is usually the first indication of an opportunity. Where you look for change is different for different businesses. Demographics is always one, and technology is always one. But if the change looks like an opportunity, you put one or two good people to work on it.

Then, with your second hand, you have to be receptive to what comes in over the transom. You have to have somebody at the top who enjoys the unexpected. The most important thing I have to tell people at the top of the organization is that they're not being paid for being clever. They're being paid for being right.

I have a friend in Canada who arrived penniless from Europe right out of a displacement camp. Today he has a $3 billion company, a leader in the high-tech field of information. He credits all of his success to his willingness to listen to customers who say, I want to show you something that we are doing.

Peter Senge: That's an appreciation of surprise. There's an element there that you're talking about, which is completely disregarded in formal management education. We're supposed to figure things out. We're supposed to make the machine work and correct problems when they come up. But when you are creating, a lot of the most important developments are what you *didn't* expect. It's how you recognize and deal with surprise that counts.

Peter Drucker: That will become absolutely crucial, because there will be a great many surprises, and if every surprise is a threat we won't be around for very long. I'm not saying that every surprise is an opportunity, but every surprise is something to be taken seriously.

Peter Senge: You need to learn how to ask, Is this a *relevant* surprise? If we were out sailing and the wind changed, that would be a surprise, but it would be a relevant surprise. We would know immediately that our prior course was not nearly as important as dealing with the surprise. The problem that happens in a lot of corporations is people immediately disregard most of the surprises as being not relevant. So how do we help people think about that distinction?

Peter Drucker: Most problems cannot be solved. Most problems can only be survived. And one survives problems by making them irrelevant because of success. It's amazing how many minor ills the healthy body can stand. One focuses on success, and especially on unexpected success. And runs with it. This is a matter, above all, of placing people.

What I have learned to do is to take a sheet and list our opportunities, and the risks. I try to focus on few priorities; one cannot do too much. And then I have a list of the best-performing, ablest people in the organization, and try to match the people to the opportunities. Until I have a name, a deadline, and accountability I have good intentions and nothing else.

Peter Senge: That's one of the most simple and basic lessons for leaders, is find where the energy wants to go, and work with it. Sometimes there's a part of us that wants to correct the people that are wrong, rather than finding the people who are passionate to build something and supporting them.

Peter Drucker: One answer to this is the human law that says the gap between the people at the top and the average is a constant. And it's terribly hard to work on that big average. You work on the few at the top and you raise them, and the rest will follow.

I knew the late Georg Solti, who raised the Chicago Symphony Orchestra in five years from comfortable mediocrity to being world class. He told me, "I looked at 128 members in the orchestra, and the 20 who were top flight and wanted to excel, and worked with them. Sure, I had to fire a second oboe or cello. But suddenly the standards, the vision had changed." One runs with performers, one runs with success.

Peter Senge: It connects back to something you mentioned earlier when you said there's no shortage of creativity in organizations. The question is, Are we paying attention to the creativity that's trying to come out? Or are we busy trying to move the whole thing in lockstep fashion?

Peter Drucker: A substantial majority of executives in all organizations spend most of their time worrying whether we need that fourth carbon copy. The weight is constantly being pushed into being program focused and mediocrity focused. One has to fight it all the time.

How do you create a balance between change and continuity?

Peter Drucker: Today's businesses, especially American businesses, are upsetting people unnecessarily—not because there is too much change, but because leaders do not even try to emphasize the continuity, the relationships, the mature responsibilities that convert them all into an organization.

Peter Senge: We tend to think that people are stressed out because there's too much change. I don't think that's true. People are stressed because they're profoundly uneasy at what it is they're doing. There's a principle in biology that I'm just starting to understand. A famous biologist, talking about the evolution of species, said history is a process of transformation through conservation. Nature preserves a small set of essential features and thereby allows everything else to change. For example, bi-lateral symmetry, whereby nature can produce 2 legs, 4 legs, 8 legs, 16 legs, is conserved across diverse species. If we start to un-derstand there's a fundamental principle that allows change to occur in nature, then we immediately see that as human beings living and working together we must continually ask the ques-tion, What do we intend to preserve?

Peter Drucker: The same biologist would probably have also said that it's by no means an accident that all animals have the same number of heartbeats during their lifetime. Whether this is a salamander or a human being, it's the same. Nature learned that this is optimum, and preserved it. And if you look at orga-nizations what is the equivalent? It is trust, and we are not really doing the things needed to preserve the trust in an organiza-tion. And trust basically means predictability.

The things you fundamentally are committed to remain the same. They are values, they are not tools. That is the way you help create trust. And on that basis you can have very rapid change and it doesn't upset people.

During a time when people's commitment to their work and their work-place is critical, how can organizations promote worker satisfaction?

Peter Senge: We tend to think that in a traditional organiza-tion people are producing results because management wants re-sults, but the essence of a volunteer organization is people who produce because *they* want the results. If people are enjoying their work, they'll innovate, they'll take risks, they'll trust one another because they are committed to what they're doing. And it's fun. Edwards Deming used to talk about people seeking joy in work. Americans thought this sounded very naive and romantic. It's always puzzled me why people think that's so strange.

Peter Drucker: No, that's anything but romantic, that's pure realism. But one reason for our attitude is clearly that legacy that work is a curse. It is amazing how quickly most people in retirement deteriorate. Work is one of the two dimensions of the human being. The other is love and family. And people who perform enjoy what they're doing. I'm not saying they like everything they do. Everybody has to do a lot of routine. I'm a professional writer and I know I have to rewrite. Nobody enjoys rewriting but it's got to be done, and I enjoy it because I enjoy the work. That is the difference, I believe, not between mediocrity and performing, but between an ordinary organization and what you call a learning organization, one where the whole organization grows.

I work with many nonprofit, pro bono communities, and my business friends and clients don't believe me when I tell them that I have learned from the nonprofit more to be applied to business than the other way around. To be sure, nonprofits have to learn to read a balance sheet, but that's easy. The things that nonprofits can do, for example, to attract and mobilize and hold volunteers, the business will have to learn with respect to knowledge workers.

Today we see so many businesses trying to duck the problem of managing the knowledge worker by bribing him with stock bonuses and options. We know from experience that works in good times, but only in good times, but then it boomerangs, terribly.

Peter Senge: You know, Peter, as I think about all the things we've talked about, it would be easy for someone to feel a bit overwhelmed in the present situation. There's not only so much changing, there's so much changing at different levels. I think we both share the sense that we're at the *beginning* of something, not the end.

Peter Drucker: People are secure if they realize that this time of sudden, unexpected, and radical change is a time of opportunity. So I'm very hopeful. No, hopeful is the wrong word; optimistic is the wrong word. The right word is excited.

Peter F. Drucker has been a teacher, writer, and adviser to senior executives for more than 50 years. Author of 31 books, including *Management Challenges for the 21st Century*, he is honorary chairman of the Drucker Foundation and Clarke Professor of Social Sciences at the Claremont Graduate University in Claremont, California.

Peter M. Senge is a senior lecturer at the Massachusetts Institute of Technology and chairman of the Society of Organizational Learning, a global community of corporations, researchers, and consultants dedicated to personal and institutional development. He is author of *The Fifth Discipline* and coauthor of *The Fifth Discipline Fieldbook* and *The Dance of Change*.

3

Lessons for
Change Leaders

Peter M. Senge

*Reflecting on his conversation with Peter Drucker, Senge
observes that the first step in thinking about the future is to
consider the givens (if A happens, B will occur). This includes recognizing long-range changes, such as demographics, and emerging industries, such as life sciences. In difficult
times, old approaches no longer work. He urges leaders to
abandon the Machine-Age mind-set and realize that: (1)
problem solving (a negative focus) is not creating (a positive
focus); (2) effective leaders do not need to control, they are
open to surprise and do not ignore the unexpected, and they
encourage diversity of thought; and (3) change starts with
a passionate few who should be encouraged, and they will
lead the rest.*

Peter Senge offers further reflections on the challenges of organizational learning, leadership, and change. Here, draw-
ing from the themes raised in a conversation with Peter Drucker
(see previous chapter, "Strategies for Change Leaders: A Conversation") and from his own work, Senge presents his observa-
tions of what it will take for leaders to be effective in the 21st
century.

A clear logic flows through Peter Drucker's comments on leadership and change. He opens the conversation by identifying basic constraints to action. He then draws out broad implications of these constraints and offers principles for guiding our choices, along with problems he anticipates along the way.

Identifying constraints is a concept that engineers know well. Others call them the *givens*. The first step in disciplined thinking about the future is to consider the givens.

That approach is at the heart of Royal Dutch Shell's scenario planning process. A key architect of that planning process, Pierre Wack, believed there was great confusion about anticipating the future. "You cannot forecast," he said, "but when it rains for a week in the foothills of the Himalayas, you know the Ganges will flood." *That* is a given.

The first constraint that Drucker describes is demographics. He's one of the few organizational thinkers who continually points to demographic change. Many managers are too impatient to consider the kind of 30- to 50-year changes Drucker describes; they're worried about the next 30 to 50 *days*. But if you're a senior executive, one of your fundamental tasks is to think longer term than others in the organization. Understanding the demographic shift that we know is occurring is like noticing the rain in the foothills of the Himalayas. It is a way to anticipate change. For instance, one forecast we can make with confidence, based on demography, is that retirement as we know it will disappear for most people in the next 20 years.

The second constraint that Drucker identifies is less widely understood. It has to do with our perception of the information revolution, which he regards as just at its outset. Moreover, he sees aspects of the great transition we are living through that go well beyond information technology.

Drucker identifies several broad implications of these constraints. First, all organizations will have to learn how to accept change. Indeed, he suggests that all must become "change leaders," or else face the future doomed to only react. Second, as this era of change continues, there may be many surprising developments—for example, emerging industries in which information technology plays an important but small part. Drucker gives the provocative example of fish farming. Third, leaders must learn to create receptivity to change by practicing the principle of abandonment, cutting loose from old practices, even before they are no longer justified economically.

He identifies several other principles that will matter: weakening the obsessive hold of problem solving in favor of creating, seeing change as an opportunity rather than a threat, and understanding that change depends on small numbers of those with passion to create something new, not on the majority. Last, he warns us of the consequences of executives who do not "enjoy the unexpected" and of the time required for basic innovation and building first-class performance.

For me, unpacking Peter's reflections starts with thinking a bit more deeply about the economic and social transition that is creating the context for leadership today. The emerging industries of the Next Economy, Drucker tells us, will have little to do with our current notions of information technology. They will have more to do with the life sciences. He reminds us that it is not technology that makes a new age of history, it is a new mind-set. Whether a technology changes the world depends on how we think about and use that technology. It is the new metaphor, not the technology per se, that transforms us.

Patterns of Change

As Josef Schumpeter observed, industrial economies evolve in waves characterized by how significant new technologies find their way into the economic system. Consider the pattern of technological innovation that has marked four great periods of change in the industrial era:

- *The 1830s.* The spread of the railroad and factory production practices coincides with the opening of the West in the United States and tremendous social dislocation.

- *The 1880s and 1890s.* Telephone and communications technology enter the economy—along with deep and sustained unemployment that reached 18 percent in 1893.

- *The 1930s.* Commercial airlines, the automobile, and the oil industry start to become dominant in the throes of the Great Depression.

- *The mid-1970s to early 1990s.* This period of economic stress also marks the real beginning of the biotech and information revolution, including the first biotech start-ups and the Internet.

The lesson to take from this pattern is simple: The shift to radically different industries and technologies is a recurring phenomenon of the Industrial Age. So the radical shifts to a "Net economy" and e-commerce, while disruptive, are not unprecedented; they are a familiar feature of the Industrial Age. Moreover, these shifts take place during the winters of economic

performance. When times are good we don't innovate. We in-
crementally improve; we look for advantage on the margin.
Why do hard times foster change? That's when dominant organizations are in disarray. They try to pump up the products and
strategies that have always sustained them, but the old reliable
approaches no longer work. The ground beneath the business and
social institutions of the era has shifted. This opens the door for
new ideas and new organizations. These epochs of change provide the context for any leader thinking about the future today.

What makes the current period so distinctive is that we are
simultaneously living through a new wave of technology and a
much longer-term phenomenon—the transition to a new age.
Most people call it the Information Age, but that is because, I
believe, they confuse the technological transition that is occurring with this deeper transition. A new age is defined by new
metaphors and core assumptions. To appreciate this, we must
reflect on the metaphors that have guided the past 200 years.

What is the dominant metaphor of the Industrial Age? *The
machine*.

At the beginning of the Industrial Age, labor productivity
had been the same for centuries. Then, in a period of 50 years
in England, it increased by a factor of 100. It was an unprecedented change. Drucker says we've lived through two epochal
periods in the past 500 years—one represented by the printing
press and the second by the steam engine. The steam engine
was the prototypical machine. It launched the Industrial Revolution, or what Russell Ackoff calls the Machine Age.

We in the West are all products of the Machine Age. We
tend to think of our organizations as machines. Why else does
it seem so natural to talk about "leaders who *drive* change"? It
is because the guiding ethic of the Machine Age is control; we

would not consider operating a machine, or "running" an organization, that we could not control.

The principles Drucker suggests are easy to describe, but they are difficult to practice because each contradicts some aspect of this Machine Age thinking.

The Case for Abandonment

If we're entering a new era of extraordinary change, Drucker believes that every organization must develop the discipline of planned abandonment. Unless we develop a discipline of shedding things, letting go, we cannot create something new. The first step in that process is to realize how hard it is.

It's difficult to abandon what we do because we are emotionally attached. Drucker tells us, "I have seen so many people who have no personality except in their product." We have emotional attachments to our work. We *are* our work. The tendency to become what we do holds for organizations as well as individuals.

To begin to abandon the old—which is what it takes to truly lead change—I believe we must embrace three other non–Machine Age strategic principles.

- Problem solving is not creating.
- Effective leaders are open to surprise.
- Change starts with the passionate few.

Problem Solving Is Not Creating

Organizational life is shaped by two fundamentally different orientations: creating versus problem solving. For most of us, problem solving dominates. Virtually our entire educational system is based on it. Most of our work as managers is about solving problems. We identify successful managers as problem solvers. And organizations that primarily define success in terms of who solves what problems create certain expectations and capabilities. This is a natural point of view if we see the world around us as being made up of machines: machines break down and need to be fixed. The trouble comes when problem solving becomes the dominant focus of the enterprise, especially in a time when we are leaving the Machine Age behind us.

When we focus only on problems we don't have time to look at possibilities. There is a fundamental difference between problem solving—making problems go away—versus creating, bringing something new into being. People in the creative arts are not confused by this distinction. For artists, writers, performers, or musicians, it doesn't matter how original your ideas are. The question is, what can you bring into reality?

Shifting from my comments on Drucker to my own thoughts on the subject, I am convinced that this question challenges our view of the organization. As products of the Machine Age, we tend to see work life as a series of things that need to be fixed. Yet most of us see the limits of this approach in our personal lives. When people are asked to identify what is most important to them, what usually comes up is family, children, parenting. Parents intuitively know that they are participating in a process of bringing something into reality. Of course, on a day-to-day or hour-to-hour basis parenting often feels like a series of problems. But we know that it is creating, helping children grow, not just the problem solving, that gives parenting such meaning and richness.

Likewise, it is creating something new, not managing day-to-day problems, that brings meaning to work life. That is the power of Drucker's observation: "It's amazing how many minor ills the healthy body can survive." It is a reminder to focus on what is important, which is to build vitality, not "solve" all disease symptoms. When we are clear about what is primary—growing healthy systems as opposed to eliminating all ailments—we're creating. Our work has meaning. When we lose that clarity, our work loses its meaning. It's that simple.

Effective Leaders Are Open to Surprise

Every organization needs to have a systematic approach to examining the future. At the same time its leaders must look for today's unexpected success. That is usually the best way to spot new opportunities.

These are what Drucker calls the right hand of disciplined thinking and the left hand of openness to surprise. He uses the phrase "being receptive to what comes in over the transom." This receptivity must start at the top. Yet few organizations are full of senior executives who enjoy the unexpected. This is not surprising. After all, who generally gets promoted in organizations? The good problem solvers, people who value predictability and control.

This poses a practical issue about how we identify and develop people for leadership positions. The fact is, most organizations, and most people, are not wired to readily perceive the unexpected. Most of us would agree that it is important for senior executives to continually scan the environment, talk to customers, get a sense of the market and the times, identify emerging trends. However, it's extraordinarily hard for us to do this.

Our perceptions of the world are based on past experience and the mechanics of cognition (see "Barriers to Seeing Differently"). Most successful organizations don't adapt to waves of change simply because they cannot see those waves coming.

That is why diversity is a core leadership issue. Ultimately this goes beyond racial, ethnic, or gender diversity, although it includes them. It has everything to do with how we see the world. I believe successful organizations of the future will work consciously to develop diversity of thought. But this will be difficult for Machine Age organizations, dominated by the tendency toward homogeneity, a norm instilled by the assembly line. Machine Age organizations tend to fall back on their established ways of seeing the world, largely because they are so homogenous in their outlook. Organizations and communities need many eyes. Only by working with people who see things differently can we be truly open to surprise.

Change Starts with the Passionate Few

Leaders (and teachers) spend too much time trying to remediate weaknesses and too little building on strengths. Remember Georg Solti, conductor of the Chicago Symphony, who found 20 musicians who had a passion to do something new: Rather than trying to push the entire organization forward, he focused on the top performers. It's an atypical strategy, but it's the most effective one. As Drucker notes, there's plenty of creativity in most organizations. We simply don't pay attention to it.

To build a strategy for change, see where the natural leadership is already surfacing in the organization. People follow their own leaders—based on excellence of performance, clarity of vision, or quality of the heart. That's the only antidote to relying on one person to direct others and hoping that person is open to the unexpected. Looking for natural leaders and seeing "where

Barriers to Seeing Differently

Why is it so difficult to spot signs of change in the environment? Why do we often fail to respond in new ways to the shifts we do see? One tool used widely within the Society for Organizational Learning network, drawn from 60 years of research in cognitive psychology and linguistics, provides some useful answers.

The Ladder of Inference is a way of thinking about what goes on when we perceive the world. It distinguishes several levels on which the mind operates and suggests ways to overcome the psychological blinders that can inhibit fresh understanding.

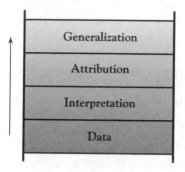

The Ladder of Inference

On the bottom rung of the ladder is *data*—information that is directly observable. For instance, Jim walked into our meeting at 9:15. Or, my boss is nodding as I speak. Based on data we immediately climb the next step on the ladder—*interpretation*: Jim is 15 minutes late. My presentation is going well. However, our interpretation of data is based largely on our culture. In Brazil, for instance, a colleague joining a 9:00 meeting at 9:15 would not be considered late. In Japan, nodding carries no implication of agreement.

From our interpretations we make *attributions*, assumptions about other people: Jim is a jerk. My boss agrees with me; she shares my values. Finally comes *generalization*—high-order inferences or stereotypes. There are, of course, professional stereotypes—"engineers can only work with other engineers"—as well as gender and racial stereotypes.

We move up the ladder at blinding speed, and we fail to distinguish the data from the interpretation from the attribution from the generalization. Based on the subtext of the conversation, we leave a meeting convinced that we're succeeding brilliantly—or failing miserably. Those are sweeping conclusions, and they constrain fresh thinking and effective change in organizations. Part of a leader's job is to identify important changes, and point to new directions. To do that, we must be aware of these constraints and build teams that bring a diverse set of interpretations to our discussions.

the energy wants to go" sounds hopelessly soft, but it is one of the toughest challenges of leadership. It means committing ourselves to cultivating leadership throughout the organization, building a culture of performance, and creating an environment where people see that their visions really matter.

But this principle likewise contradicts Machine Age thinking. It seems much more "natural" to leaders to think in terms of change programs and roll-outs.

The New Metaphor

The underlying shift that I believe is needed if we are to follow the principles that Drucker prescribes is to think of our organizations as living organisms rather than machines. We must study the way nature innovates. Nature does not fix broken systems. Nature creates the new in the midst of what already exists. In nature things always start small and grow in response to favorable conditions and self-directed energy. No one controls living systems, and their pattern of development is always characterized by surprise and serendipity. The science of the 21st century is dramatically different from the science of the Machine Age. It's a science of living systems and it is giving us the new metaphors we need to make sense of a changing world.

One of the great illusions of the Machine Age is that everything can be speeded up. Bill O'Brien, the retired CEO of Hanover Insurance, says, "It takes nine months to have a baby. It doesn't matter how many people you put on the job." You cannot speed up everything. You can send an e-mail message to 30 people, but will they read them—and even more important, will they think about them? That's one of the rude awakenings of our time. The innovation process is fundamentally human and social. It's been with us for millennia. Like natural processes, it has limits to how much it can be speeded up.

The Last Constraint

Ultimately, in addition to demography and old mind-sets, we face a third constraint and a powerful force for change. Every day, on average, 200 times the body weight of every American is extracted from the earth to support our standard of living. Ninety-nine percent of that material will end up in a junk heap. We have created the most wasteful economic system in the history of humankind. It is not, in current form, a sustainable system. We are running into environmental *and* social constraints. The Machine Age has not been an age that cares much about equity. For much of it, particularly over the past 25 years, it has been characterized by increasing concentration of wealth and income. That too is probably not sustainable.

As Pierre Wack reminds us, when it rains in the foothills of the Himalayas for seven days, the Ganges will flood. How much longer can we create inequity and destroy species? Will it change in the next 10 or 20 years? Can we continue to run our organizations in the future as we have in the past? Those are the kinds of questions that leaders will have to answer.

The question facing us today is, Are we in the middle of the next wave in the Machine Age or is it really the beginning of something new? Technology will not determine that. It can at best only enable it. It will be determined by us—by our values, our commitments, our passions, and, in the end, our perseverance and patience.

Peter M. Senge is a senior lecturer at the Massachusetts Institute of Technology and chairman of the Society of Organizational Learning, a global community of corporations, researchers, and consultants dedicated to personal and institutional development. He is author of *The Fifth Discipline* and coauthor of *The Fifth Discipline Fieldbook*, *The Dance of Change*, and *Schools that Learn*.

4

Leading Transition

A New Model for Change

William Bridges and Susan Mitchell

Change requires a state of transition—a psychological re-orientation. Transition happens more slowly than change and entails three processes: (1) saying goodbye to old ways that made people successful in the past and are part of their work identities; (2) shifting into neutral, coping with uncertainties, and coming to grips with what they are being asked; and (3) moving forward and behaving in a new way. The neutral zone is uncomfortable; it offers the potential for regression or precipitous action. But leaders can employ certain practices to help people through transition.

Change is nothing new to leaders, or their constituents. We understand by now that organizations cannot be just endlessly "managed," replicating yesterday's practices to achieve success. Business conditions change and yesterday's assumptions and practices no longer work. There must be innovation, and innovation means change.

Yet the thousands of books, seminars, and consulting engagements purporting to help "manage change" often fall short. These tools tend to neglect the dynamics of personal and organizational transition that can determine the outcome of any change effort.

As a result, they fail to address the leader's need to coach others through the transition process. And they fail to acknowledge the fact that leaders themselves usually need coaching before they can effectively coach others.

In years past, perhaps, leaders could simply order changes. Even today, many view it as a straightforward process: establish a task force to lay out what needs to be done, when, and by whom. Then all that seems left for the organization is (what an innocent-sounding euphemism!) *to implement the plan*. Many leaders imagine that to make a change work, people need only follow the plan's implicit map, which shows how to get from here (where things stand now) to there (where they'll stand after the plan is *implemented*). "There" is also where the organization needs to be if it is to survive, so anyone who has looked at the situation with a reasonably open mind can see that the change isn't optional. It is essential.

Fine. But then, why don't people "Just Do It"? And what is the leader supposed to do when they Just *Don't* Do It—when people do not make the changes that need to be made, when deadlines are missed, costs run over budget, and valuable workers get so frustrated that when a headhunter calls, they jump ship?

Leaders who try to analyze this question after the fact are likely to review the change effort and how it was implemented. But the details of the intended change are often not the issue. The planned outcome may have been the restructuring of a group around products instead of geography, or speeding up product time-to-market by 50 percent. Whatever it was, the change that seemed so obviously necessary has languished like last week's flowers.

That happens because transition occurs in the course of every attempt at change. Transition is the state that change puts people into. The *change* is external (the different policy, practice, or structure that the leader is trying to bring about), while *transition* is internal (a psychological reorientation that people have to go through before the change can work).

The trouble is, most leaders imagine that transition is automatic—that it occurs simply because the change is happening. But it doesn't. Just because the computers are on everyone's desk doesn't mean that the new individually accessed customer database is transforming operations the way the consultants promised it would. And just because two companies (or hospitals or law firms) are now fully "merged" doesn't mean that they operate as one or that the envisioned cost savings will be realized.

Even when a change is showing signs that it may work, there is the issue of timing, for transition happens much more slowly than change. That is why the ambitious timetable that the leader laid out to the board turns out to have been wildly optimistic: it was based on getting the *change* accomplished, not on getting the people through the *transition*.

Transition takes longer because it requires that people undergo three separate processes, and all of them are upsetting.

Saying goodbye. The first requirement is that people have to let go of the way that things—and, worse, the way that they themselves—used to be. As the folk wisdom puts it, "You can't steal second base with your foot on first." You have to leave where you are, and many people have spent their whole lives standing on first base. It isn't just a personal preference you are asking them to give up. You are asking them to let go of the way of engaging or accomplishing tasks that made them successful in the past. You are asking them to let go of what feels to them like their whole world of experience, their sense of identity, even "reality" itself.

On paper it may have been a logical shift to self-managed teams, but it turned out to require that people no longer rely on a supervisor to make all decisions (and to be blamed when things go wrong). Or it looked like a simple effort to merge two work groups, but in practice it meant that people no longer worked with their friends or reported to people whose priorities they understood.

Shifting into neutral. Even after people have let go of their old ways, they find themselves unable to start anew. They are entering the second difficult phase of transition. We call it *the neutral zone*, and that in-between state is so full of uncertainty and confusion that simply coping with it takes most of people's energy. The neutral zone is particularly difficult during mergers or acquisitions, when careers and policy decisions and the very "rules of the game" are left in limbo while the two leadership groups work out questions of power and decision making.

The neutral zone is uncomfortable, so people are driven to get out of it. Some people try to rush ahead into some (often *any*) new situation, while others try to backpedal and retreat into the past. Successful transition, however, requires that an organization and its people spend some time in the neutral zone. This time in the neutral zone is not wasted, for that is where the creativity and energy of transition are found and the real transformation takes place. It's like Moses in the wilderness: it was there, not in the Promised Land, that Moses was given the Ten Commandments; and it was there, and not in the Promised Land, that his people were transformed from slaves to a strong and free people (see "Lessons from the Wilderness").

Today it won't take 40 years, but a shift to self-managed teams, for instance, is likely to leave people in the neutral zone for six months, and a major merger may take two years to find its way

Lessons from the Wilderness

Even a great leader like Moses faced a trying test of his leadership in the neutral zone. But he was up to the task, so take note of some of his methods:

Magnify the plagues. To make the old system (Pharaoh) "let go" of his people, Moses called down plagues—and didn't stop until the old system gave way. At this stage, problems are your friend. Don't solve them; they convince people that they need to let go of the old way.

Mark the ending. What a symbolic "boundary event" Moses had! After his people crossed the Red Sea, there was no turning back!

Deal with the "murmuring." Don't be surprised when people lose confidence in your leadership in the neutral zone: Where are we going? Does he know the way? What was ever wrong with Egypt, anyway? In periods of transition, look for opportunities to have contact with the individuals in transition; distance will be interpreted as abandonment. And show your concern for them by engaging them in conversation about the issues that are most on their minds; you may think there are more important things to talk about, but *they* don't think so.

Give people access to the decision makers. Moses (aided by his OD specialist, Jethro) appointed a new cadre of judges in the wilderness to narrow the gap between the people and the decision makers.

Capitalize on the creative opportunity provided by the neutral zone. It was in the wilderness, not in the Promised Land, that the big innovation took place: the Ten Commandments were handed down. It will be in the neutral zone that many of your biggest breakthroughs occur.

(continued on the next page)

> *Resist the urge to rush ahead.* It seems as though little is happening in the neutral zone, but this is where the transformation is taking place. Don't jeopardize it by hurrying.
>
> *Understand that neutral-zone leadership is special.* Moses did not enter the Promised Land. His kind of leadership fit the neutral zone, where things are confusing and fluid. But it was Joshua who could lead in the more settled state of the Promised Land. A literal new leader isn't needed, though, just a new style of leadership. Establishing a new beginning requires a much more logical approach, with an appeal to the followers' understanding, while the fluidity and ambiguity of the neutral zone makes an emotional connection between the leader and the followers more critical.

out of the neutral zone. The *change* can continue forward on something close to its own schedule while the *transition* is being attended to, but if the transition is not dealt with, the change may collapse. People cannot do the new things that the new situation requires until they come to grips with what is being asked.

Moving forward. Some people fail to get through transition because they do not let go of the old ways and make an ending; others fail because they become frightened and confused by the neutral zone and don't stay in it long enough for it to do its work on them. Some, however, do get through these first two phases of transition, but then freeze when they face the third phase, the new beginning. For that third phase requires people to begin behaving in a new way, and that can be disconcerting—it puts one's sense of competence and value at risk. Especially in organizations that have a history of punishing mistakes, people hang back during the final phase of transition, waiting to see how others are going to handle the new beginning.

Helping Leaders to Lead Change

Understanding the transition process is a requirement for almost any senior executive. However, it is when the organization is in transition that leaders themselves often need help. They are so close to the changes that have been launched that they may fail to

- Remember that they themselves took some time to come to terms with the necessary change—and that their followers will need at least as long to do so (see figure)

- Understand why anyone would not embrace change, and so believe that their followers are ignorant, rigid, or outright hostile to the new direction

- See that it is the *transitions*, not necessarily the changes themselves, that are holding people back and thereby threatening to make their change unworkable

Most leaders come from backgrounds where technical, financial, or operational skills were paramount, and those skills provide little help when it comes to leading people through transition. Such leaders may be pushing the limits of their understanding of the future, and they need perspective and advice. That is where a trusted colleague, confidant, coach, or consultant can offer valuable counsel to the leader. This person's background or professional affiliation can vary widely; what matters is that she or he understands how to help people through transition. It is a role that is far more interpersonal and collaborative than is played by most consultants or trainers accustomed to teaching a skill or prescribing a solution.

The higher leaders sit in an organization the more quickly they tend to move through the change process. Because they can see the intended destination before others even know the race has begun, senior managers often forget that others will take longer to make the transition: letting go of old ways, moving through the neutral zone, and, finally, making a new beginning.

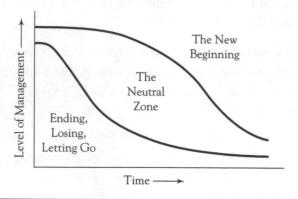

The Marathon Effect

No training program can prepare a leader for managing a transition. Yet no leader can effectively lead change—which is what leadership is all about—without understanding and, ultimately, experiencing—the transition process. What leaders need, instead, is individualized assistance whereby they learn to

- Create plans to bring their followers through the particular transition they face—not through generic "change." A trainer can teach leaders a generalized approach ("The Ten Steps . . ."), but a good coach can help leaders discover their own best approaches.

- Work with their own goals, limitations, and concerns to create a development plan that prepares them for the future.

Times of transition are becoming the rule rather than the exception. Yet few leaders know how to prepare for the challenges that lie ahead. Transition leadership skills must be congruent with, must capitalize and build on, the leader's own strengths and talents. They cannot be found in a set of theoretical leadership skills.

The transition adviser works collaboratively with each leader to assess the leader's place in the three-part transition, the strengths the leader brings and how to leverage them, and what the current situation demands. It is a personal and completely customized process.

A Method for Managing Transition

Although the details of a transition management plan are unique to each situation, the adviser must help a leader with the following essential steps:

1. Learn to describe the change and why it must happen, and do so succinctly—in one minute or less. It is amazing how many leaders cannot do that.

2. Make sure that the details of the change are planned carefully and that someone is responsible for each detail, that time lines for all the changes are established, and that a communications plan explaining the change is in place.

3. Understand (with the assistance of others closer to the change) just who is going to have to let go of what—what is

ending (and what is not) in people's work lives and careers—
and what people (including the leader) should let go of.

4. Make sure that steps are taken to help people respectfully
let go of the past. These may include "boundary" actions (events
that demonstrate that change has come), a constant stream of information, and understanding and acceptance of the symptoms
of grieving, as well as efforts to protect people's interests while
they are giving up the status quo.

5. Help people through the neutral zone with communication
(rather than simple information) that emphasizes connections
with and concern for the followers. To keep reiterating the "4 P's"
of transition communications:

The *purpose:* Why we have to do this

The *picture:* What it will look and feel like when we
reach our goal

The *plan:* Step by step, how we will get there

The *part:* What you can (and need to) do to help us
move forward

6. Create temporary solutions to the temporary problems
and the high levels of uncertainty found in the neutral zone. For
example, one high-tech manufacturer, when announcing a plant
closing, made interim changes in its reassignment procedures,
bonus compensation plans, and employee communications processes to make sure that displaced employees suffered as little as
possible, both financially and psychologically. Such efforts should
include transition monitoring teams that can alert the leader to
unforeseen problems—and disband when the process is done.

7. Help people launch the new beginning by articulating the
new attitudes and behaviors needed to make the change work—

and then modeling, providing practice in, and rewarding those behaviors and attitudes. For example, rather than announcing the grandiose goal of building a "world-class workforce," leaders of transition must define the skills and attitudes that such a workforce must have, and provide the necessary training and resources to develop them.

Coaching for Change

Since the ability to manage transition is tied to the realities of an actual leader in an actual situation, mutual trust between adviser and leader is essential. Only that way can leaders be honest enough to bring their fears and concerns to the surface quickly, hear what the situation is really "saying" rather than focusing on a program that a consultant is trying to sell, and gain the personal insight and awareness of the transition process that can be carried into the future.

Because this transition management relationship is a close and ongoing one, the adviser gets to know the leader's situation well and follows it as it changes. Understanding the dynamics of transition is far removed from the kind of leadership training most organizations provide. Traditional trainers and consultants seldom possess such intimate knowledge of their client. Whatever personal coaching they provide is usually subsumed in the teaching of a generic skill or body of knowledge. And because the relationship is time-limited, there is a natural pressure to produce quick, clear results.

However, because transition advisers work within the context of the situation at hand, their focus is not on how to "be a leader" or even how to "change an organization" but on how to provide the particular kind of leadership that an organization in

transition demands. For that reason, the results of the relationship are very specific: the development of new skills and behaviors geared to the needs of the unique time and circumstances
in which the person leads.

New Models of Leadership

Once you understand transition, you begin to see it everywhere.
You realize that many of the issues commonly addressed as leadership, learning, or organizational development challenges are
really an inevitable part of transition. Indeed, in today's organizations, without experiencing and successfully managing a difficult transition, no leader can be effective for very long. That
suggests reinventing most models of leadership development.
The best leadership development programs implicitly address
the challenge of understanding change—they are experiential,
tailored to the needs of the leader, and based on delivering real-
world results. But most could be strengthened by explicit attention to transition management.

The final lesson that the process of transition holds for leadership development is that the relationship between adviser and
leader is not much different from that between a leader and the
people that she or he "leads." We treat that word ironically because the leadership that is appropriate to a modern, fast-moving
organization—where work is based on task and mission rather
than job description, and is distributed among contributors inside and outside the organization—takes on a new meaning. It is
not the drum-major-at-the-head-of-the-parade leadership appropriate to yesterday's organization; it is the give-and-take, person-
centered leadership by which the sports coach gets the best effort
out of each member of a team.

The kind of leadership most effective today is similar to the kind of service that the best consultant gives a client: collaborative assistance that is both problem-solving and developmental. Its target is both the situation and the professional capability of the person. Today's leader, in a fundamental sense, is a coach, and the leader can best learn that role by being coached.

William Bridges is a writer and principal of William Bridges & Associates. He helps individuals and organizations deal more effectively with change. He has published nine books, including *Managing Transition*, *JobShift*, and *Creating You & Co*. The *Wall Street Journal* has named him one of the top ten executive development presenters in the United States.

Susan Mitchell, principal of Mitchell Consulting Group, specializes in leadership development, executive coaching, performance management, and team development. She has worked with leading industrial and professional service organizations and has held senior line management positions with international consulting and training firms.

5

The Enduring Skills of Change Leaders

Rosabeth Moss Kanter

Kanter states that people must be given the time, the respon-sibility, and the resources to implement lasting change. Keys to mastering change are the imagination to innovate (con-cepts), the professionalism to perform (competence), and the openness to collaborate (connections). Leaders must collect information and monitor the organization's external environ-ment; challenge the prevailing wisdom; assess what doesn't fit; communicate a compelling need for change with passion and conviction; build coalitions with people who have the abil-ity to make things happen; have patience and persevere; transfer ownership of the change to workers; and support, coach, provide resources, and reward accomplishments.

Hundreds of books and millions of dollars in consulting fees have been devoted to leadership and organizational change. No issue of the past 15 years has concerned more man-agers or a wider spectrum of organizations. Yet, for all the at-tention the subject merits, we see every day that certain kinds of change are simple. If you're a senior executive, you can order budget reductions, buy or sell a division, form a strategic alli-ance, or arrange a merger.

Such bold strokes do produce fast change, but they do not necessarily build the long-term capabilities of the organization. Indeed, these leadership actions often are defensive, the result of a flawed strategy or a failure to adapt to changing market conditions. They sometimes mask the need for a deeper change in strategy, structure, or operations, and they contribute to the anxiety that accompanies sudden change.

Years of study and experience show that the things that sustain change are not bold strokes but long marches—the independent, discretionary, and ongoing efforts of people throughout the organization. Real change requires people to adjust their behavior, and that behavior is often beyond the control of top management. Yes, as a senior executive, you can allocate resources for new product development or reorganize a unit, but you cannot order people to use their imaginations or to work collaboratively. That's why, in difficult situations, leaders who have neglected the long march often fall back on the bold stroke. It feels good (at least to the boss) to shake things up, but it exacts a toll on the organization.

Forces for Change

Organizational change has become a way of life as a result of three forces: globalization, information technology, and industry consolidation. In today's world, all organizations, from the Fortune 500 to the local nonprofit agency, need greater reach. They need to be in more places, to be more aware of regional and cultural differences, and to integrate into coherent strategies the work occurring in different markets and communities.

The first two forces for change—globalization and technology—will inevitably grow. But it's not enough for organizations to simply "go international" or "get networked." In a global, high-tech world, organizations need to be more fluid, inclusive, and responsive. They need to manage complex information flows, grasp new ideas quickly, and spread those ideas throughout the enterprise. What counts is not whether everybody uses e-mail but whether people quickly absorb the impact of information and respond to opportunity.

Industry consolidation, *the* business story of 1998–99, has a less certain future. But even if that trend abates, the impact of mergers, acquisitions, and strategic alliances will be felt for years. Mergers and acquisitions bring both dangers and benefits to organizations (see "Innovating in the Age of Megamergers"). Partnerships, joint ventures, and strategic alliances can be a less dramatic but more highly evolved vehicle for innovation. However, you must not starve an alliance or a partnership. You have to invest the time and resources to work out differences in culture, strategy, processes, or policies.

You also have to bring together people at many levels to talk about shared goals and the future of the alliance in general, not just their small functional tasks. Many alliances unravel because, while there is support at the top of the organization, departments at lower levels are left to resolve tensions, answer questions, or fill gaps on their own. The conflicts and wasted efforts that result can end up destroying value instead of creating it. You have to make sure that the goals of people at many levels of the organizations are aligned, and that people get to know each other, before you can expect them to build trust.

Keys to Mastering Change

Change is created constantly and at many levels in an organization. There is the occasional earthshaking event, often induced by outside forces; there are also the everyday actions of people

Innovating in the Age of Megamergers

Do mergers and acquisitions impair innovation? It depends on the nature of the deal and the abilities of leaders. Some consolidations, such as the effectively managed merger of Sandoz and Ciba Gigy to form Novartis, are growth-oriented. In that case, most of the pieces that were combined and eventually sold off were in the chemical business. What remained was a new, strategically coherent life sciences company. It can grow by building new knowledge and collecting in one place a set of diverse products that previously had been scattered.

The key for leaders in a growth-oriented merger—where the aim is to tackle new markets and do things together that could not be done separately—is to foster communication, encourage involvement, and share more knowledge of overall strategy, special projects, and how the pieces of the new entity fit together.

On the other hand, many mergers are aimed primarily at reducing capacity and cutting costs. That is the case in most of the recent banking and financial services mergers, for instance. These consolidations, and the efficiencies that result, can make good economic sense. Yet massive organizational change often drains so much time and energy that the sustainable benefits of the long march are lost, and the temptations of the bold stroke are irresistible. Often this leaves leaders with the task of putting the best face on what, for many employees, is not a promising future.

Mergers that focus on cost cutting—often necessary to pay for the deal and to satisfy the demands of shareholders—can threaten the funding of promising experiments and disrupt innovation. Massive mergers can also drive out the knowledge that fuels innovation.

> Merged organizations often lose a degree of staff professionalism because people resent losing a voice in their destiny or having to do tasks that they're not prepared for. Training budgets and opportunities for collegial exchange also tend to shrink. Most consolidations fail to create more integrated, value-adding enterprises and fall short of their promised benefits. That is what makes them such a demanding test of leadership.

engaged in their work. In change-adept organizations, people simply respond to customers and move on to the next project or opportunity. They do not necessarily change their assumptions about how the organization operates, but they continuously learn and adapt, spread knowledge, share ideas. By making change a way of life people are, in the best sense, "just doing their jobs."

Change-adept organizations share three key attributes, each associated with a particular role for leaders.

- *The imagination to innovate.* To encourage innovation, effective leaders help develop new *concepts*—the ideas, models, and applications of technology that set an organization apart.

- *The professionalism to perform.* Leaders provide personal and organizational *competence*, supported by workforce training and development, to execute flawlessly and deliver value to ever-more-demanding customers.

- *The openness to collaborate.* Leaders make *connections* with partners who can extend the organization's reach, enhance its offerings, or energize its practices.

These intangible assets—concepts, competence, and connections—accrue naturally to successful organizations, just as they do to successful individuals. They reflect habits, not programs—personal skills, behavior, and relationships. When they are deeply ingrained in an organization, change is so natural that resistance is usually low. But lacking these organizational assets, leaders tend to react to change defensively and ineffectively. Change compelled by crisis is usually seen as a threat, not an opportunity.

Mastering deep change—being first with the best service, anticipating and then meeting new customer requirements, applying new technology—requires organizations to do more than adapt to changes already in progress. It requires them to be fast, agile, intuitive, and innovative. Strengthening relationships with customers in the midst of market upheaval can help organizations avoid cataclysmic change—the kind that costs jobs and jolts communities. To do that, effective leaders reconceive their role—from monitors of the organization to monitors of external reality. They become idea scouts, attentive to early signs of discontinuity, disruption, threat, or opportunity in the marketplace and the community. And they create channels for senior managers, salespeople, service reps, or receptionists to share what customers are saying about products.

Classic Skills for Leaders

The most important things a leader can bring to a changing organization are passion, conviction, and confidence in others. Too often executives announce a plan, launch a task force, and then simply hope that people find the answers—instead of offering a dream, stretching their horizons, and encouraging people to do the same. That is why we say, "leaders go first."

However, given that passion, conviction, and confidence, leaders can use several techniques to take charge of change rather than simply react to it. In nearly 20 years of working with leaders I have found the following classic skills to be equally useful to CEOs, senior executives, or middle managers who want to move an idea forward.

1. *Tuning in to the environment.* As a leader you can't possibly know enough, or be in enough places, to understand everything happening inside—and more importantly outside—your organization. But you can actively collect information that suggests new approaches. You can create a network of *listening posts*—a satellite office, a joint venture, a community service. Rubbermaid operates its own stores, for instance, even though it sells mostly to Wal-Mart and other big chains. These stores allow the company to listen to and learn from customers. Likewise, partnerships and alliances not only help you accomplish particular tasks, they also provide knowledge about things happening in the world that you wouldn't see otherwise.

Look not just at how the pieces of your business model fit together but at what *doesn't* fit. For instance, pay special attention to customer complaints, which are often your best source of information about an operational weakness or unmet need. Also search out broader signs of change—a competitor doing something differently or a customer using your product or service in unexpected ways.

2. *Challenging the prevailing organizational wisdom.* Leaders need to develop what I call kaleidoscope thinking—a way of constructing patterns from the fragments of data available, and then manipulating them to form different patterns. They must question their assumptions about how pieces of the organization, the marketplace, or the community fit together. Change

leaders remember that there are many solutions to a problem and that by looking through a different lens somebody is going to invent, for instance, a new way to deliver health care.

There are lots of ways to promote kaleidoscopic thinking. Send people outside the company—not just on field trips, but "far afield trips." Go outside your industry and return with fresh ideas. Rotate job assignments and create interdisciplinary project teams to give people fresh ideas and opportunities to test their assumptions. For instance, one innovative department of a U.S. oil company regularly invites people from many different departments to attend large brainstorming sessions. These allow interested outsiders to ask questions, make suggestions, and trigger new ideas.

3. *Communicating a compelling aspiration.* You cannot sell change, or anything else, without genuine conviction, because there are so many sources of resistance to overcome: "We've never done it before." "We tried it before and it didn't work." "Things are OK now, so why should we change?" Especially when you are pursuing a true innovation as opposed to responding to a crisis, you've got to make a compelling case. Leaders talk about communicating a vision as an instrument of change, but I prefer the notion of communicating an *aspiration.* It's not just a picture of what could be; it is an appeal to our better selves, a call to become something more. It reminds us that the future does not just descend like a stage set; we construct the future from our own history, desires, and decisions.

4. *Building coalitions.* Change leaders need the involvement of people who have the resources, the knowledge, and the political clout to make things happen. You want the opinion shapers, the experts in the field, the values leaders. That sounds obvious,

but coalition building is probably the most neglected step in the change process.

In the early stages of planning change, leaders must identify key supporters and sell their dream with the same passion and deliberation as the entrepreneur. You may have to reach deep into, across, and outside the organization to find key influencers, but you first must be willing to reveal an idea or proposal before it's ready. Secrecy denies you the opportunity to get feedback, and when things are sprung on people with no warning, the easiest answer is always no. Coalition building requires an understanding of the politics of change, and in any organization those politics are formidable.

When building coalitions, however, it's a mistake to try to recruit everybody at once. Think of innovation as a venture. You want the minimum number of investors necessary to launch a new venture, and to champion it when you need help later.

5. *Transferring ownership to a working team.* Once a coalition is in place, you can enlist others in implementation. You must remain involved—the leader's job is to support the team, provide coaching and resources, and patrol the boundaries within which the team can freely operate. But you cannot simply ask managers to execute a fully formed change agenda; you might instead develop a broad outline, informed by your environmental scan and lots of good questions, from which people can conduct a series of small experiments. That approach not only confers team ownership, but allows people to explore new possibilities in ways that don't bet the company or your budget.

As psychologist Richard Hackman has found, it is not just the personalities or the team process that determine success; it's whether or not the team is linked appropriately to the resources they need in the organization. In addition, leaders can allow teams to forge their own identity, build a sense of membership, and enjoy the protection they need to implement changes. One of the temptations leaders must resist is to simply pile responsibility on team members. While it is fashionable to have people wear many hats, people must be given the responsibility—and the time—to focus on the tasks of change.

6. *Learning to persevere.* My personal law of management, if not of life, is that everything can look like a failure in the middle. One of the mistakes leaders make in change processes is to launch them and leave them. There are many ways a change initiative can get derailed (see "Sticky Moments in the Middle of Change"). But stop it too soon and by definition it will be a failure; stay with it through its initial hurdles and good things may happen. Of course, if a change process takes long enough you have to return to the beginning—monitor the environment again, recheck your assumptions, reconsider whether the proposed change is still the right one. Abdicating your role undermines the effort because, unlike bold strokes, long marches need ongoing leadership. Most people get excited about things in the beginning, and everybody loves endings, especially happy endings. It's the hard work in between that demands the attention and effort of savvy leaders.

7. *Making everyone a hero.* Remembering to recognize, reward, and celebrate accomplishments is a critical leadership skill. And it is probably the most underutilized motivational tool in organizations. There is no limit to how much recognition you can provide, and it is often free. Recognition brings the change cycle to its logical conclusion, but it also motivates people to attempt change again. So many people get involved in and contribute to changing the way an organization does things that it's

Sticky Moments in the Middle of Change— and How to Get Unstuck

Every idea, especially if it is new or different, runs into trouble before it reaches fruition. However, it's important for change leaders to help teams overcome four predictable—but potentially fatal—roadblocks to change.

• *Forecasts fall short.* You have to have a plan—but if you are doing something new and different, you should not expect it to hold. Plans are based on experience and assumptions. When attempting to innovate, it is difficult to predict how long something will take or how much it will cost (you can predict, however, that it will probably take longer and cost more than you think). Change leaders must be prepared to accept serious departures from plans. They must also understand that if they hope to encourage innovation it is foolish to measure people's performance according to strictly planned delivery.

• *Roads curve.* Everyone knows that a new path is unlikely to run straight and true, but when we actually encounter those twists and turns we often panic. Especially when attempting to make changes in a system, diversions are likely, and unwelcome.

It's a mistake to simply stop in your tracks. Every change brings unanticipated consequences, and teams must be prepared to respond, to troubleshoot, to make adjustments, and to make their case. Scenario planning can help; the real message is to expect the unexpected.

• *Momentum slows.* After the excitement and anticipation of a project launch, reality sinks in. You do not have solutions to the problems you face; the multiple demands of your job are piling up; the people you have asked for information or assistance are not

(continued on the next page)

returning your calls. The team is discouraged and enmeshed in conflict. It is important to revisit the team's mission, to recognize what's been accomplished and what remains, and to remember that the differences in outlook, background, and perspective that now may divide you will ultimately provide solutions.

• *Critics emerge*. Even if you have built a coalition and involved key stakeholders, the critics, skeptics, and cynics will challenge you—and they will be strongest not at the beginning but in the middle of your efforts. It is only then that the possible impact of the change becomes clear, and those who feel threatened can formulate their objections. This is when change leaders—often with the help of coalition members, outside partners, or acknowledged experts—can respond to criticism, remove obstacles, and push forward. Tangible progress will produce more believers than doubters.

important to share the credit. Change is an ongoing issue, and you can't afford to lose the talents, skills, or energies of those who can help make it happen.

Today's organizations have come to expect bold strokes from their leaders. Sometimes these are appropriate and effective—as when a project or product that no longer works is put to rest. But bold strokes can also disrupt and distract organizations. They often happen too quickly to facilitate real learning, and they can impede the instructive long marches that ultimately carry an organization forward. That is why imagination, professionalism, and openness are essential to leadership, not just to leading change. They give organizations the tools to absorb and apply the lessons of the moment.

Likewise, techniques that facilitate change within organizations—creating listening posts, opening lines of communication, articulating a set of explicit, shared goals, building coalitions, acknowledging others—are key to creating effective partnerships and sustaining high performance, not just to managing change. They build the trust and commitment necessary to succeed in good times or in bad. Even periods of relative stability (unusual for most organizations) require such skills.

Change has become a major theme of leadership literature for a good reason. Leaders set the direction, define the context, and help produce coherence for their organizations. Leaders manage the culture, or at least the vehicles through which that culture is expressed. They set the boundaries for collaboration, autonomy, and the sharing of knowledge and ideas, and give meaning to events that otherwise appear random and chaotic. And they inspire voluntary behavior—the degree of effort, innovation, and entrepreneurship with which employees serve customers and seek opportunities.

Increasingly, the assets that cannot be controlled by rule are most critical to success. People's ideas or concepts, their commitment to high standards of competence, and their connections of trust with partners are what set apart great organizations. All these requirements can be enhanced by leaders, but none can be mandated. For all the upheaval of the past 15 years, that may be the biggest change of all.

Rosabeth Moss Kanter is the Ernest L. Arbuckle Professor of Business Administration at Harvard Business School. She is former editor of the *Harvard Business Review*, a consultant to major corporations around the world, and author of 15 books, including *Rosabeth Moss Kanter on the Frontiers of Management*, and, most recently, *Evolve! Succeeding in the Digital Culture of Tomorrow*.

6

Managing
Segment Zero

Andrew S. Grove

---

*Strategic Inflection Points, Grove's term for describing mon-
umental changes in the way an organization does business,
are indicated when a significant entity shifts, a key collabo-
rator changes, or people begin talking about things that no
one had heard of a year before. Knowing what is happening
outside an organization is crucial, as is the ability to note dissonance between strategic statements and strategic actions,
which tend to reflect new realities. Moving an organization
from denial to acceptance of change and then to action involves experimenting and tolerating the disruption, allowing people to adapt, picturing the new organization, and
doing away with established practices.*

Major change in the competitive landscape can take many
forms. It may be the introduction of new technologies,
a new regulatory environment, or a sudden shift in customer
preferences. But the change usually hits the organization in
such a way that those of us in senior management are among
the last to notice.

Such monumental changes represent what I call Strategic Inflection Points—events that cause you to fundamentally change

61

your business strategy. At such moments in the life of an organization, nothing less will do.

The biggest difficulty with Strategic Inflection Points—aside from the havoc they create—is distinguishing them from the many changes that routinely impinge on your business. Obviously, not every change we respond to requires a dramatic reaction. But the answers to three questions may signal the onset of such a change:

- *Has the company or the entity that you most worry about shifted?* I have a mental "silver bullet" test. If you had one bullet, what would you shoot with it? If you change the direction of the gun, that is one of the signals that you may be dealing with something more than an ordinary shift in the competitive landscape.

- *Is your key complementor—a company whose work you rely on to make your product more available—changing?* A shift in direction by a partner or market ally can be as decisive as a move by a competitor.

- *Do the people you have worked with for 20 years seem to be talking gibberish?* Are they suddenly talking about people, products, or companies that no one had heard of a year before? If so, it's time to pay attention to what's going on.

Strategic Inflection Points occur in organizations every day, but of course they are much easier to spot in hindsight. Consider three cases from telecommunications, retailing, and computing:

The 1984 breakup of the Bell system. The telecommunications industry has changed in more fundamental ways than anybody could have imagined 15 years ago. Yet the real impact of the change is not what happened in the industry but what happened *outside* it. Telecommunications services became very different from the standpoint of the business buyer; you suddenly had to make a multitude of purchase decisions, and make different vendors' products work together.

The rise of superstores. Local booksellers have been shaken to the core by the likes of Barnes & Noble and Borders.

The introduction of PCs. Desktop computers transformed the computing business—yet the manufacturers of mainframes were the last to understand the impact of this change.

Knowing Something Is Up

Although these changes were profound, just a few years later these industries are again being upended by a new set of Strategic Inflection Points.

In 1996, the Telecommunications Act was derided by many as inconsequential—but something must have changed because since its passage between $150 billion and $200 billion worth of mergers and acquisition have taken place or are pending: MCI and WorldCom; SBC and Pacific Telesis and Ameritech; Bell Atlantic and Nynex and GTE; TCI and AT&T.

In retailing, Barnes & Noble has been eclipsed by Amazon.com. In just two years the Internet-based upstart has achieved a market value greater than Barnes & Noble and Borders combined. Barnes & Noble seems to recognize that its world has changed, because it is pushing into online sales as well—in fact, it is underselling its own stores online.

Even when senior executives miss the external signs of change, we often have evidence under our noses that something is happening. One thing to look for in an organization in the throes of change is a growing dissonance between its strategic statements and its strategic actions. Of the two, strategic actions are usually the first to reflect new realities, because strategic actions are driven by the competition, by the sales force, by the sheer necessity of winning in the marketplace day in and day out. It is often a long time before the collective impact of those actions is translated into a reformulation of the company's stated strategy.

We have a phrase at Intel that says a lot about us: "Don't argue with the emotions, argue with the data." But sometimes you have to argue against the data because the data are pertinent to your past, not your future. Tomorrow's Strategic Inflection Point may not even register in your data.

Because such signs of change are not data-driven, debate between senior managers, technologists, and members of the sales force often become emotional. It is important at such times to listen to the people who bring you bad news, and to know that those people are often in the lower ranks of the organization. Unless you welcome their contrarian views—and learn to live with the fear that such views can bring—you will never hear from those useful Cassandras who can help you respond quickly to major change.

Phases of Change

As you try to make sense of the new landscape, it is important to move the organization quickly from denial to acceptance of change. Moving toward acceptance—and from there to action— usually involves two phases. First, you must experiment and let chaos reign. That's important because you are not likely to restructure your organization at the first sign of trouble. Rather, you have to let the business units deal with and adapt to change—

and while they do so you have to watch and learn from them. You watch the dissonance that grows in the company, and you think about how to close it—by changing both what you do and what you say you do. Most important, you use this period of experimentation to picture the shape of the new industry and how it will look at the end of these changes.

As this chaotic period resolves, you enter the second phase of change, which I describe as the Valley of Death. Doing away with established practices and established people—tearing apart before you can put together something new—is not fun.

One of the disciplines necessary in any organization with finite resources (which is every organization) is the ability to balance every new effort against current commitments. In other words, the "yeses" have to equal the "nos." Nothing challenges leadership as much as managing the balance between the yeses—which everyone is happy to add to the balance sheet—and the nos, which no one ever volunteers for.

It is also wise to refrain from talking too much about these climatic shifts in the early stages. Talking prematurely about changes that disrupt people's lives and are not truly believed in can undermine your efforts before they have a chance to work. But once they are in place, it is essential for leadership to speak clearly about what the changes are about and what the organization is going to do. At this point, hopefully, the other side of the Valley of Death is clear, and you can describe the future that lies ahead.

The Rise of Segment Zero

These difficult organizational passages represent an attempt to innovate—or to respond to the disruptive innovations of a competitor. In *The Innovator's Dilemma* Harvard Business School

Professor Clayton Christensen looks at how quickly and quietly a new market strategy or new technology can challenge an established industry—and how market leaders tend to dismiss such challenges as otherwise unworthy of serious attention. But Christensen's thesis is simple: What matters is, is the new approach good enough for the market? Does it satisfy a market demand? Long-term success depends on a market's reaction to phenomena that are "good enough."

Christensen provides vivid evidence of this process in the growth of the minimills at the expense of the large, integrated steel mills. The integrated mills supply many segments of the steel market—from high-end steel plate to structural steel to the lowest end of the market, rebar. But in the late 1970s, low-cost minimills started providing small amounts of steel that was relatively poor quality, but was good enough for rebar.

The steel companies said, in effect, "Who cares? That's a rough, low-margin business. Let them have it." The story would end there, except that the minimills continually improved their quality—and in short order took bites out of every segment of the market, including steel plate.

Rebar offers a lesson to every business: the overlooked, underserved, and seemingly unprofitable end of the market can provide fertile ground for massive competitive change. However, the bottom of the market often doesn't figure into the market leader's strategy.

In a classic market model, a company might compete in four market segments (see figure). In Intel's case, these had ranged from the huge but low-margin consumer market (Segment 1) to the small but lucrative market for network servers (Segment 4). What was missing from our model was the market for computers costing less than $1,000. I call it Segment Zero because until recently its value was negligible.

Intel's standard market model (top) worked well for years. But the company has now changed its strategy to respond to a large, previously uncharted market segment.

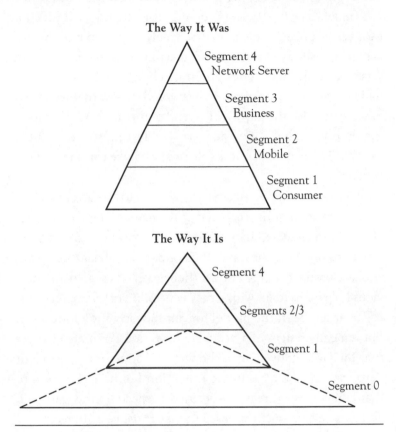

The Way It Was

Segment 4
Network Server

Segment 3
Business

Segment 2
Mobile

Segment 1
Consumer

The Way It Is

Segment 4

Segments 2/3

Segment 1

Segment 0

Rebuilding the Pyramids

Low-cost PCs had been around for years. They provided poor performance, limited features, and usually required upgrading to do what people wanted. They failed in the market, and most people in the industry considered them a joke. But while we weren't looking, these machines created a new market and grew—from less than 5 percent of the U.S. desktop market in 1994 to about 20 percent in late 1998.

The low-cost trend was influenced by excess capacity and falling prices for memory chips, and more recently by a PC price war (induced by the Asian economic crisis) that shaved $100 off the average price of a computer. Suddenly we had to face the disturbing possibility that the four-segment market model that had served us well for decades might be changing. Low-cost PCs had become the rebar of our industry, and we saw that we would have to fight for the growing low end of the market by competing on price. That is not necessarily a lasting strategy, but it worked. The bad news is it accelerated what we call the product waterfall.

The waterfall represents the way we used to operate: Introduce a microprocessor at the high end of the market, then a year later offer it in the middle, then, finally, at the low end of the market. The transition from the top to the bottom took about three years, and as a product trickled down the market, it created an enormous hole for us to fill with a new generation of microprocessor.

That has been the model for our industry for a long time. But remember, signs of a Strategic Inflection Point are changes that fundamentally change the way you do business. Segment Zero was, in fact, a Strategic Inflection Point. To respond to that competitive threat, we decided to speed up the waterfall. Today, a new product that used to take three years to reach the bottom of the market gets there in 12 to 18 months.

That means Segment Zero products, which failed in the past because they were always yesterday's product, have become *good enough*. The processors that we introduced in January 1997, for instance, trickled down to Segment Zero by the end of 1997. And even in the computer industry it's difficult to call a machine that you marketed as world-class in January obsolete in December.

Thus, in a matter of months, we had to completely change how we operated. We stopped arguing with the data. We segmented our products much more finely. We began to change managerial attitudes, cost structures, and the whole product line. We had to revisit our fundamental belief systems. And one of the new principles we had to accept is that prices do not go up, because we helped create that reality. Once prices do not go down, we are likely to have to live with them. We had to realize, most of all, that we cannot paint all segments of the market with the same brush. Using a single product strategy—even one as elegant as the waterfall—would no longer work.

After all, the PC used to be one thing; that is no longer the case. Network servers have different characteristics, different manufacturers, different customers, and different customer value sets from other machines. In addition, we saw that each of our major segments—consumer, mobile, business, and server—was becoming more fragmented. Each could be divided into at least two subsegments, with distinct value sets. Thus we needed to design each product for the target segment, rather than simply reproducing the same product a year later.

We put 650 engineers to work on a separate Segment Zero product line based on our best ideas for delivering what those customers wanted. We were able to reduce the cost of a product while maintaining its functionality because, as technology improves, we can put more transistors on a chip. Ordinarily, we use that increased capacity to improve the performance of chips. We continue to do that for the high-performance segment. But we can also use extra components to reduce the manufacturer's cost of the total PC, not just the cost of the chip, by integrating additional functions on the same chip. Technically, this makes perfect sense. We simply had never done it before because we never considered Segment Zero part of our market.

Once we segmented our product strategy, we also had to segment our brand strategy. In three years the Intel Pentium processor had become one of the strongest brand names in the world. Yet, as part of our segmentation strategy, we broke our reliance on the Pentium processor brand for all segments of the market. We now use the Pentium II Xeon processor for the high-end server market and the Celeron processor for the basic PC, which requires different products and a different identity.

Can we repeat the market performance of the original Pentium? Can we afford to aggressively market two different brands? Are we going to confuse the marketplace? There are more questions than we can answer, and it would have been easy for us to say, "Let's just play it safe and hang on to the brand that we established." But that was not a viable option.

Accepting Market Reality

Through all these strategic changes, one principle has served us well. We realized long ago that in our industry, you must price your product to the market and that cost must follow price. We reaffirmed our belief in this principle and made cost reduction a priority. By legitimizing Segment Zero, we have accepted the market, and the market in turn has reached deep inside our factories, pushing us to cut costs dramatically. However, managerial attitudes also had to change. Just two years ago we were in denial about Segment Zero; now we have a dedicated team to service it, and we pursue that market with the cost fanaticism that our industry has always employed.

The Segment Zero phenomenon is not just a computing phenomenon, nor just an Intel phenomenon. It was evident in the compact segment of the car industry in the 1970s. It is clearly at work today as the Internet becomes a major force in all kinds of businesses. Online trading, for instance, is affecting every major brokerage house. It is a lower-cost, poorer-quality alternative to full-service trading, but clearly it is good enough for millions of investors. And good enough is often enough to remake an industry.

Not every low-cost product represents a Segment Zero phenomenon. Not every low-cost alternative is good enough to pay for, or has a chance of getting better, or is likely to be embraced by a significant portion of the buying population. But Segment Zero does create a powerful opportunity for new market leaders to emerge. These new leaders have no stake in sheet steel, or high-cost PCs, or brick-and-mortar bookstores; they can put all of their efforts into market innovation. They pose a huge challenge to the incumbent and demand a quick and serious response.

Andrew S. Grove is chairman of Intel Corporation and served as its president and CEO for more than 10 years. Trained as a chemical engineer, Grove has lectured at Stanford University Graduate School of Business and is author of numerous articles and four books, including the best-selling *Only the Paranoid Survive*. He has been honored as CEO of the Year, Technology Leader of the Year, and, in 1997, *Time*'s Person of the Year.

7

Management by Commitments

Donald N. Sull

Transformational commitments to change can help leaders break free from behaviors that no longer are useful. The commitment may be to a course of action (such as a new product or major acquisition), to an ambitious goal (often stated in terms of market share), to stretch relationships (such as by linking with leading-edge customers, partners, or investors), or to an operating philosophy (a guiding statement of how the organization will move into the future).

Most leaders today recognize that the future will differ profoundly from the past, and that competitive formulas that led to earlier success can lead to future disaster. History, however, exerts a strong gravitational pull on organizations, particularly successful ones. Faced with dramatic changes in their competitive environment, most companies respond not by doing things differently but by doing more of what worked before. When these tried-and-true actions fail to achieve the desired results, most companies redouble their efforts, and in their haste to dig themselves out of a hole only dig themselves in deeper.

I call this tendency to respond to dramatic shifts in the environment by accelerating past activities "active inertia"—and have observed the phenomenon across many industries, countries, and historical eras. Organizations fall into active inertia because their mental models, organizational routines, relationships with key stakeholders, and underlying values wear deep grooves that channel future behavior. An organization's past, as a result, can largely determine its future.

How then can managers break free from the strong gravitational pull of the past? Transformational commitments provide one powerful lever. They allow a leader to break from the status quo by increasing the costs or eliminating the possibility of persisting in past behaviors.

Transformational commitments differ fundamentally from the operational commitments—such as budget agreements, job assignments, or customer guarantees—that occupy much of a manager's day-to-day routine. While making and honoring routine commitments is necessary to maintaining the status quo, transformational commitments require leaders to step outside the confines of their usual practices and commit to change.

A promise to achieve an ambitious objective—what Jim Collins and Jerry Porras describe in *Built to Last* as "Big Hairy Audacious Goals"—is the most familiar type of transformational commitment. President Kennedy's pledge to land a man on the moon by the end of the 1960s is the archetypical example. Commitment to achieving a goal is not, however, the *only* type of transformational commitment, nor is it always the most effective. Leaders struggling to transform their organizations can choose from four distinct types of commitments—to a course of action, to an ambitious goal, to "stretch relationships," or to an operating philosophy. Each type of commitment offers certain advantages and limitations in breaking from the trajectory of the past.

Types of Commitments

Commitment to a course of action. Many leaders transform their organizations by committing to a course of action that represents a sharp break with the past. Consider the case of Asahi Breweries. For nearly two decades, Asahi controlled only 10 percent of the Japanese beer market, dwarfed by market leader Kirin's 60 percent share. Asahi's small size prevented it from achieving economies of scale in production, distribution, or marketing, and Asahi averaged returns only one-fifth of those enjoyed by Kirin. Asahi managers cut costs by using cheap hops and malt, which diminished taste and further depressed sales. Asahi's persistent underperformance attracted a hostile takeover bid and necessitated a layoff of 17 percent of the workforce— unprecedented events in 1980s corporate Japan.

When Hirotaro Higuchi became Asahi's president in 1986, he recognized that the company could never succeed through cost cutting alone. Instead Higuchi committed Asahi to a clear course of action by investing heavily to expand the company's capacity to produce dry beer, an alternative to the lager that had dominated the Japanese beer market for decades. Although it was initially unclear whether early demand for dry beer represented a fad or a fundamental shift in consumer preferences, Higuchi bet heavily on dry and increased Asahi's capacity fourfold between 1986 and 1990. That large investment deterred competitors from adding capacity and convinced skeptical retailers that the company would do everything possible to make dry beer succeed. In the end, Asahi's bet paid off, allowing the company to overtake Kirin and emerge as Japan's leading brewer.

Commitment to a course of action typically takes the form of a new product introduction, capacity expansion, or major acquisition. Such actions can transform a company by refocusing attention—from cost-cutting to growth through product differ-entiation in the case of Asahi. These highly visible actions pro-vide a laserlike focus throughout the organization and signal management's confidence in the chosen direction. Large com-mitments to a new course of action can also increase employees' motivation to make the action pay off. By betting heavily on a single move—Asahi's total investment in dry beer exceeded the company's book assets—a manager can exhaust the resources re-quired to pursue an alternative strategy. Like a general who burns the bridges behind his advancing army, a leader who commits to a course of action can motivate others by dramatically raising the costs of failure.

Commitment to an ambitious goal. Managers can also break out of historical patterns of behavior by committing to achieve an ambitious goal, often stated in terms of market share (think GE's mandate to be No. 1 or 2 in every market) or in terms of over-taking the industry leader (recall Komatsu's rallying cry to "beat Cat" as it attempted to overtake Caterpillar). While a commit-ment to a course of action specifies exactly what a company will do, a commitment to a goal specifies only what a company plans to achieve, not how.

Compaq's dramatic trajectory for most of the 1990s illus-trates how a commitment to achieving an ambitious goal can help a company overcome inertia—and can also put the orga-nization at risk. In the wake of his abrupt dismissal in 1999, CEO Eckhard Pfeiffer may be remembered as a leader who over-reached. But in fact he delivered remarkable results in his eight-year tenure. When Pfeiffer replaced founder Ron Canion as CEO in 1991, Compaq was foundering. Pfeiffer reengineered the company's product development, manufacturing, and dis-tribution processes to slash costs. He also committed to making

Compaq the No. 1 U.S. PC maker by 1996, although it was a distant fifth in the market, selling only one-quarter the volume of industry leader IBM at the time. Pfeiffer's commitment to industry leadership succeeded brilliantly in focusing the organization. Compaq employees woke up every morning knowing exactly what to do that day—ship more boxes. The company overtook IBM two years ahead of plan. Its market value increased from $2 billion in 1991 to $42 billion in 1997, when *Forbes* magazine honored Compaq as its company of the year and placed Pfeiffer on the cover.

The clarity of Pfeiffer's target aligned the organization around a common goal, and its audacity rallied the troops. Commitments to achievement allow flexibility in how to pursue the desired end. They are most effective in improving a company's position in a well-established industry relative to well-known competitors.

Commitment to stretch relationships. While most leaders are familiar with "stretch goals" as a management tool, few recognize the power of *stretch relationships* in overcoming inertia. Managers commit to stretch relationships by linking their firm's fortunes to leading-edge customers, accomplished partners, sophisticated investors, or demanding employees. Most managers avoid stretch relationships because they disrupt the status quo by placing "unreasonable" demands on the organization. It is just such demands, however, that pull the organization—sometimes kicking and screaming—from its past. By seeking out and committing to these relationships, leaders prevent their organizations from slipping back into bad habits.

Consider Infosys Technologies. India's leading software company, Infosys has enjoyed 17-fold growth in revenues from 1994 to 1999. The inertia of established business practices in India has historically frustrated aspiring entrepreneurs, many of whom have emigrated to pursue their dream elsewhere. However, CEO N. R. Narayana Murthy succeeded in part by committing to relationships with leading-edge customers. Infosys managers carefully "recruit" customers based on their sophistication, prestige, and potential for a long-term relationship. Infosys clients read like a Who's Who of admired companies including Nortel, Nordstrom, Xerox, and GE. Nearly all of its clients are headquartered outside India. By committing to ongoing relationships with sophisticated global customers, Infosys helped establish software as one of India's few globally competitive sectors.

Infosys was also the first Indian company to list its stock on an American stock exchange. Infosys listed on Nasdaq to increase its visibility in the United States and issue stock to lure American employees; other companies have listed on U.S. exchanges to attract sophisticated investors. While these listings of course provide access to America's deep capital markets, savvy managers can also harness their relationships with investors to overcome corporate inertia.

Between 1997 and early 1999, for example, 35 European companies listed on the New York Stock Exchange, joining Germany's Hoechst, Italy's ENI, and Finland's Nokia. France's Groupe Danone, a world leader in dairy products, biscuits, and bottled water (Evian), listed the company on the New York Stock Exchange in 1997. While other European leaders were hiding from active investors, CEO Franck Riboud actively sought them out. Riboud used the resulting capital market pressure to transform Danone by setting targets for each business based on return on capital and paying managers bonuses up to 70 percent of their salaries based on economic value added.

Committing to binding relationships with leading-edge customers or investors can provide a powerful mechanism for overcoming inertia. These relationships provide an unrelenting external focus by exposing employees to best practices and world-class performance expectations. Commitments to relationships rather than specific actions or achievements also allow companies ample flexibility to improvise. Infosys evolved from low-value-added activities like testing and maintaining software to serving mission-critical systems. Stock market pressures can also help managers overcome the inertia of legacy businesses. To focus Danone's sprawling empire, Riboud rapidly divested several underperforming businesses—including some purchased by his father, who preceded him as CEO.

Commitment to an operating philosophy. Managers attempting to overcome inertia can commit to an operating philosophy that differs from their organization's traditional way of proceeding. "Operating philosophy," as I use the term, is not a detailed list of rules and regulations, nor a compilation of platitudinous values, but rather a concise statement of *how* an organization will move into an uncertain future. Cisco, for example, states its operating philosophy as "to listen to customer requests, monitor all technological alternatives, and provide customers with a range of options from which to choose." Cisco's operating philosophy guides employees while leaving sufficient flexibility to respond to shifts in customer demands and technology.

McKinsey & Company illustrates how a leader can transform a company by committing to an alternative operating philosophy. Today McKinsey numbers among the world's most admired companies, but in the 1940s McKinsey, Wellington and Partners was one of dozens of fledgling accounting and engineering firms peddling advice to managers. Marvin Bower, a partner in the New York office, grew convinced that practices grounded in the firm's accounting heritage were ill-suited to the demands of the new consulting sector.

Trained as a lawyer, Bower worked with other partners to articulate an operating philosophy based on the more established professions of law and medicine. As McKinsey faced the challenges of rapid growth, global expansion, and changing markets, Bower constantly reaffirmed the firm's commitment to the "professional approach" and initiated and guided dialogues among his partners about what professionalism meant in practice. In attracting and retaining the best staff, for example, McKinsey explicitly adopted the legal model of hiring freshly minted graduates and promoting them on an up-or-out policy. Bower even borrowed the language of the established professions, insisting that McKinsey had "clients" not "customers," "professionals" not "workers," and was a "firm" rather than a "company." Even today, McKinsey translates professionalism into concrete guiding principles such as "develop and excite our people through active apprenticeship and stretching, entrepreneurial opportunities," and "uphold the obligation to dissent." Other preeminent service firms such as investment bank Goldman Sachs demonstrate a similar commitment to the professional operating philosophy.

Committing to an operating philosophy is particularly well suited to firms like Cisco that face uncertain and rapidly changing environments. Hewlett-Packard's well-known "HP Way," for example, embraces concrete practices, including management by walking around, management by objective, and an open door policy. Or consider IBM's remarkable transformation. When Lou Gerstner took over the floundering company in 1993, he famously quipped that the last thing IBM needed was a vision. While Gerstner didn't set concrete targets, he did define a clear way of proceeding: IBM would return to its roots and provide customers with integrated solutions. This simple philosophy allowed Gerstner and his team to recognize the value of retaining all of IBM's divisions rather than splitting the company up into "Baby Blues." Gerstner's operating philosophy also helped IBM identify the importance of services sooner than its competitors.

Avoiding the Commitment Trap

It is important to understand the risks inherent in each approach—and to know when to avoid making a particular commitment.

A *commitment to a course of action* can yield a huge payoff if the envisioned future comes to pass, as it did for Asahi. But what if dry beer had proven to be a passing fad? Asahi would have been saddled with massive excess capacity and no resources to pursue alternatives. A major commitment to a single course of action can sharply curtail a company's flexibility when responding to unexpected events, and represents a risky approach for companies facing rapid change and an uncertain future.

A *commitment to achieving an ambitious goal* is also risky if the competitive landscape is shifting faster than the organization can reach its target. Such commitments can lock a company into "tunnel vision"—the determination to achieve a clear objective despite an uncertain environment. Tunnel vision can focus managers so completely on the target that it obscures the peripheral vision needed to observe subtle shifts in the environment. Consider Microsoft, which despite its vaunted market prowess was a latecomer to the Internet—and nearly paid a high price for missing the party. The company's intense focus on PCs when developing Windows 95 played to its strength in desktop computing—but distracted managers from early signs of the Internet's growing importance, thereby providing Netscape an opportunity to dominate the early Web browser market.

Tunnel vision can also lull employees into believing that simple answers are always possible, thereby blunting their tolerance for ambiguity. After Compaq became No. 1, employees continued to demand a clear goal, even as the company moved into a turbulent era of e-commerce, free PCs, and information appliances like the Palm Pilot and Nokia Communicator. When Pfeiffer was unable to provide a simple vision for an uncertain world, the company lost traction, the board lost patience, and the CEO lost his job.

Likewise, while *commitments to stretch relationships* can drive continuous renewal in a company, this strategy carries its own risks. Relationships, even with leading-edge customers, employees, investors, or suppliers, can harden into ties that bind. Apple Computer, for example, succeeded by hiring dedicated engineers and attracting sophisticated customers such as desktop publishers. However, as Intel's IBM-compatible chips came to dominate the market, Apple's loyal constituents resisted attempts to move closer to a perceived enemy. While Apple has recently made up much lost ground, the company missed the early opportunity to place its superior operating system on the Intel chip.

A *commitment to an operating philosophy* can degenerate in two distinct ways. Operating philosophies can harden into detailed procedures and stifling process manuals. They can also soften into gooey value statements that provide little direction and could be used to justify any conceivable course of action. To prevent a philosophy from falling into these traps, leaders must constantly reinvigorate and redefine their philosophy in light of changing circumstances. IBM's top management, for example, reinterpreted the commitment to solving customers' problems as providing e-commerce solutions.

Choosing Your Commitments

All leaders need to weigh strategically the benefits and risks of the commitments they make. To assess whether commitment to a particular action, goal, relationship, or philosophy is likely to overcome the weight of corporate inertia, leaders can ask themselves three broad questions (see "The Three Cs of Transformational Commitments"): Is your commitment concrete? Is it credible? Is it courageous?

For instance, Hirotaro Higuchi made his commitment concrete, credible, and courageous by investing heavily in capacity for dry beer—exhausting the resources necessary to pursue alternative actions. But how can you decide which type of commitment best suits your situation? There are no hard-and-fast rules, but a few guidelines can help leaders choose wisely.

Betting on a single course of action. Staking the company's future on a single outcome makes sense if there is nothing to lose. Asahi, for example, faced bankruptcy or acquisition unless management acted decisively. A big bet also makes sense when the payoff is large. In the race to create an industry standard, for instance, the winner takes all, and the disproportionate gain may justify betting the company to come in first. AT&T's bet on cable, which exceeded $100 billion in late 1999, is such an example.

Shooting for an ambitious goal. Commitment to an ambitious goal helps companies improve their standing relative to well-known competitors in an established industry. While these commitments are dangerous in turbulent markets such as e-commerce or telecommunications equipment, they may prove useful for more stable industries such as steel, cement, and tire manufacturing, or fast food and cleaning services, where historical competitors are likely to remain your chief rivals.

The Three Cs of Transformational Commitments

To test the vitality of a commitment you are considering, ask yourself these questions:

Is your commitment concrete? The appropriate level of concreteness will depend on the nature of the commitment. A commitment to an action or goal must be more concrete than a commitment to a stretch relationship or an operating philosophy. There are, however, questions that can help solidify a commitment: Who is committing? What are they committing to? Can you quantify the commitment's impact? What milestones will trigger a review of progress? How will you measure success or failure?

Although it is difficult to assess whether a commitment is sufficiently concrete, it is much easier to determine when it is too vague. A "no" answer to any of the following questions suggests trouble: Can you articulate the commitment from memory? Can anyone else in your organization, especially on the front line, articulate it? Can you give three concrete examples of actions in accordance with your commitment? Can you give three examples of attractive opportunities that your commitment would exclude?

Is your commitment credible? Leaders must give their commitment teeth by increasing the costs of failing to honor the commitment. Some, like Higuchi, increase the costs by taking dramatic actions that are difficult to reverse.

Most managers, however, increase the credibility of their commitment by publicly staking their personal reputation and their company's reputation on honoring the commitment. In evaluating whether your commitment is credible, you can ask the following questions: Who knows about this commitment? Have you stated it publicly? Is this commitment consistent with your past behavior? What are the costs to your company of failing to honor the commitment? What are the costs to you personally of failing to honor the commitment?

Although the commitments discussed here bind the entire organization, they are still made by individuals. The congruence between their personal values and their public commitments enabled leaders like Marvin Bower and Lou Gerstner to consistently "walk the talk." A leader should ask the following questions before committing his or her organization: How deep is my personal commitment? Is this commitment consistent with my past performance and my personal values? Can I give specific examples of how I have changed my own behavior as a result of this commitment?

Is your commitment courageous? There is a great temptation to respond to organizational inertia with incremental improvements. The transformational power of commitment lies, however, in the ability to break with the past, and that requires courage. The following questions may help you assess whether your commitments are sufficiently courageous: What happens if you don't make this commitment? Are you going for gold—or hiding in the pack? Do you measure your commitment by progress toward the future or distance from the past? Is this commitment a quantum leap for your organization or an incremental change? Could you do it faster and sooner? What hinders you?

Hitching your company to a relationship. Committing to cutting-edge customers, demanding investors, or highly mobile employees can be a powerful mechanism to refocus attention or gain expertise. These commitments are particularly appropriate for forcing an introverted company to look outward. Commitments to relationships also work well when leaders can clearly articulate what most needs to change and how the new relationship will help. Riboud saw that Danone's biggest problem was historical investments in unproductive assets, and he saw that capital market pressure could provide the impetus to disentangle Danone from its legacy.

Steering with an operating philosophy. Commitment to a philosophy is particularly well suited to rapidly changing markets or business models. In times of turbulence, managers may find it safer to commit to how they will compete rather than to specific actions, goals, or relationships. This approach requires a tremendous effort from top management to ensure that the operating philosophy doesn't degenerate into overly detailed procedure manuals at one extreme or hopelessly vague clichés at the other.

Changing Leaders to Change Commitments

Often a manager's past commitments pose the greatest obstacle to future vitality. Leaders succeed by articulating a clear vision of the future and making promises consistent with that vision to customers, employees, investors, and partners. These promises are critical to win stakeholders' support, but over time they accumulate and become ties that bind leaders to a fading vision. Many manufacturers, for example, have built Web sites but then failed to publicize them to avoid alienating their established distribution partners.

Committing to the future often requires breaking historical commitments. But changing commitments of a leader's own making entails a loss of face and credibility. Thus senior executives and boards often find they must change the players to change the commitments—an observation with serious implications for promotion decisions. Executives may need to hire and promote people from outside the core business unencumbered by past practices. Divisions geographically distant from headquarters are particularly fertile grounds, as are emerging growth businesses located in a cutting-edge market.

Making the right strategic commitments is one of leaders' most important and difficult responsibilities. As a leader, you must look in the mirror and honestly ask whether you yourself can break with past promises to commit fully to a different future. Good leaders make and honor commitments, but great leaders also know when to make way for the future.

Donald N. Sull is assistant professor of strategy and international management at the London Business School and assistant professor of business administration at Harvard University. He speaks and writes extensively on business strategy and adaptation to market change. His articles have appeared in *Harvard Business Review, European Management Journal,* and the *Financial Times.*

8

The Age of Connective Leadership

Jean Lipman-Blumen

Leaders must learn to integrate interdependence and diversity. Interdependence (e.g., strategic alliances and networks) involves overlapping visions, mutual problems, and common goals. Diversity reflects the distinctive character of individuals, groups, and organizations and promotes differing priorities. Connective leaders perceive common ground and possibilities. They negotiate, persuade, and integrate. They construct networks and coalitions and collaborate with competitors to accomplish mutual goals. They have six important strengths: (1) ethical political savvy; (2) authenticity and accountability; (3) a politics of commonalities; (4) thinking long-term, acting short-term; (5) leadership through expectation; and (6) a quest for meaning.

On the cusp of a new era, Václav Havel reminds us that "Something is on the way out, and something else is painfully being born." The detritus of failed leadership is everywhere: nations divided, governments distrusted, corporations discredited, leaders discarded, and constituents disillusioned. Criticism of political, corporate, educational, even religious leaders grows. Our discomfort stems from a sea change in the conditions of leadership imposed by the new global environment. This change requires new ways of thinking and working. Most important, it makes traditional forms of leadership increasingly untenable.

Economist John Kenneth Galbraith suggests that the distinguishing feature of all great leaders is their ability to deal with the anxieties and tensions of their times. Today, two opposing tensions—interdependence and diversity—increasingly shape our world. They are transforming the circumstances under which leaders must lead. Only leaders who can confront and constructively integrate these tensions will succeed.

Understanding Interdependence and Diversity

Interdependence, driven largely by technology, connects everyone and everything, everywhere. It drives us toward collaboration in many guises—in joint ventures, partnerships, strategic alliances, networks, and temporary coalitions. Interdependence focuses on overlapping visions, mutual problems, and common goals. It seeks out similarities, fostering convergence of interests.

In contrast to interdependence, diversity concerns the distinctive character of individuals, groups, and organizations. Reflecting the human need for identity, diversity highlights everyone's uniqueness, underscoring differences and emphasizing independence and individualism. It is a force for social, economic, and cultural differentiation.

In its fullest expression, diversity is evident throughout the world—from emerging and splintering nations to fragmenting religious groups and political parties. It's a major force in the growth of single-issue political groups. In every case, diversity promotes new and often opposing priorities.

Leading in the Connective Era

Interdependence and diversity distinguish the current Connective Era, in which everyone and everything are intertwined. The importance of diversity and the inevitability of interdependence require a more fully developed leadership repertoire. Such a model—a connective leadership model—can help leaders make use of the most positive aspects of diversity and interdependence.

Connective leaders easily "get" the connections among diverse people, ideas, and institutions, even when the parties themselves do not. They perceive connections and possibilities where traditional leaders and long-term opponents see only separation and hostility. Because connective leaders can discern common ground, they can begin to address common problems. Unlike individualistic leaders before them, connective leaders can see the overlap between their own visions and those of other leaders. Eventually, through joint action on even small problems, stereotypes of opponents soften, empathy sprouts, and the common ground expands.

Connective leaders negotiate, persuade, and integrate antagonistic groups. They reach out to long-standing adversaries in order to accomplish mutual goals. Mikhail Gorbachev's rapprochement with his country's Cold War adversary exemplifies another aspect of this new leadership approach. In the unfolding Connective Era, leaders will need to engage in many forms of collaboration—even with traditional competitors. Connective leaders contribute to others' successes and act as mentors, without losing their ability to compete, take charge, and make tough independent decisions when necessary.

Connective leaders do much more: They construct and call upon social networks and multiple, shifting coalitions. They open these networks to colleagues. They seek active constitu-ents, unshackled by orthodoxy, who can share the burdens of leadership but feel free not to support the leader's every issue.

To achieve results in an era caught in the grip of interde-pendence and diversity, connective leaders must develop at least six important leadership strengths:

1. *Ethical Political Savvy.* Connective leaders have abundant political savvy; they exhibit system know-how seasoned with a strong sense of ethics. They adroitly use themselves, others, and all the resources they can garner as instruments for accomplish-ing their goals. They employ these resources overtly, ethically, and altruistically through a strategy of "denatured Machiavel-lianism." This political savvy is the secret weapon that connec-tive leaders use to couple the counter forces of diversity and interdependence.

Connective leaders use other people's personal strengths, as well as their networks, to solve group problems—not to enhance their own power. They connect emotionally with constituents through dramatic, unexpected symbols and counterintuitive gestures. Moreover, connective leaders amplify their supporters' abilities and ensure their loyalty by entrusting them with chal-lenging tasks. In the process, they spur the personal growth of those entrusted. Negotiation and persuasion are part of their po-litical repertoire. So is the ability to build shifting coalitions, using their own and colleagues' supporters.

Traditionally, we have rejected the instrumental use of oth-ers as "unethical manipulation." Nonetheless, divested of self-promotion, instrumental political know-how is especially relevant to a complex, diverse, and interdependent world. In a single week in 1993, Mary Robinson, then president of Ireland, reached out to Britain's Queen Elizabeth and Sinn Fein president Gerry

Adams. Despite immediate criticism, her historic connective visit to West Belfast set the tone for a subsequent thaw between Britain and the Irish Republican Army.

2. *Authenticity and Accountability*. When leaders consistently dedicate themselves to the purposes of the group rather than to the enhancement of their own power, they demonstrate authenticity. Authenticity establishes credibility and sustains supporters' faith in leaders. This is crucial when the leader's behavior seems confusing or contradictory—as it may in an increasingly complex world. Authenticity helps constituents determine whether the change in a leader's behavior reflects a new, more complete understanding of the problem or simply a waffling from weakness. Thus authenticity helps stem the corrosion of cynicism.

Accountability, authenticity's twin imperative, involves two major obligations: first, to explain one's decisions and actions, and second, to be held responsible before a widening jury of stakeholders. Accountability means that a leader is willing to have every choice scrutinized. Coupled with authenticity, accountability blocks unethical, irresponsible, or simply thoughtless action. In the Connective Era, a diverse set of constituents expects full disclosure, making accountability a requirement for leaders.

To be sure, connective leaders are not saints. They can be as difficult as anyone in authority. Like the rest of us, they can suffer depression when things go awry. They sometimes explode in anger. At times, they may exasperate their supporters. Generally, however, the special capacities they bring to the leadership table overshadow their human failings.

3. *A Politics of Commonalities*. In a world connected by technology but fragmented by the forces of diversity, connective leaders foster community. They do so by practicing a politics of commonalities, which offers membership to the broadest set

of constituents. They create an environment in which many constituents achieve at least part of their agenda.

To build community in organizations, connective leaders take the broadest perspective on what is needed and by whom. They search for similarities and common ground, even among groups who see their agendas as mutually exclusive. For example, a connective leader could probably convince feminists and conservatives to collaborate against pornography and domestic violence, which both groups oppose for their own separate reasons.

Similarly, the joint efforts of avowed enemies Israeli Prime Minister Yitzhak Rabin and Palestinian leader Yasser Arafat to initiate a peace process took their respective supporters by surprise. Such action is not without risk—it cost Rabin his life and nearly toppled Arafat. In each case, the leaders were in jeopardy from their own confused supporters, who mistook their connective gestures for betrayal or weakness.

Because the Connective Era is just beginning, many constituents are still locked in to traditional leadership expectations. Thus leaders who engage in connective behavior will need to communicate their intentions to constituents carefully and clearly.

Connective leaders understand the importance of reaching out to multilayered coalitions, not simply to embedded elites. When community consists of individuals from such diverse backgrounds, their divergent agendas create a social jigsaw puzzle. It takes leaders who have the skill to bevel the agendas of multiple coalitions to make the pieces fit.

4. *Thinking Long-Term, Acting Short-Term.* Day-to-day performance pressures notwithstanding, building community requires an appreciation of obscured long-term possibilities. It takes vision and courage to choose between current demands of

key constituents and a better future for a larger community. When former San Francisco mayor (now U.S. Senator) Dianne Feinstein committed scarce funds to retrofit Candlestick Park against earthquakes, she offended various groups who pressed "more urgent" demands. Later, when the Loma Prieta earthquake struck at the opening of a 1989 World Series game, 60,000 people escaped injury in the strengthened stadium.

Cherishing the future requires that leaders set aside their egos to ensure that talented people succeed them. Grooming a large cadre of potential successors is the only sure path to achieve this goal. With the possible exception of promoting clones of themselves, traditional leaders have rarely had much interest in this. In fact, they often consume their potential heirs, as both Henry Ford and his grandson demonstrated at Ford Motor Company. Succession mechanisms are commonly lacking in organizations with leaders who have little yen for bringing others into the leadership circle. Connective leaders, who coach and encourage their younger associates, are more likely to take this leadership responsibility seriously.

5. *Leadership Through Expectation.* Connective leaders set high expectations and then entrust their own most valued tasks to others. Moving beyond empowerment, they scrupulously avoid micromanaging. Instead, they stand back and rely upon the principle of reciprocation, whereby the gift of the leader's confidence is usually repaid by the constituent's outstanding performance. Connective leaders encourage the creative expansion of their vision, requiring only that the associate act ethically and legally. Beyond that, the associate's creativity can expand to its own natural limit.

Leadership through expectations is no panacea. Colleagues may misinterpret or mishandle a leader's intention. Connective leaders, however, are attuned to the dynamics of learning and recognize that not all new ventures result in immediate success. They support associates despite occasional failures and encourage them to try again. For example, one senior executive in a high-tech company routinely hosts a dinner to recognize the best "near miss" of the quarter.

6. *A Quest for Meaning.* Most people seek to leave a legacy, to be remembered for making a difference. With growing maturity, we sense the shortening of time, the need to make our lives count for something worthwhile. Altruistic, life-expanding enterprises—be they the building of an organization or a social movement—offer us such possibilities. Even as they search for their own ennobling experiences, leaders can guide others through these complicated, life-enhancing challenges. Investment banker Robert Fisher, managing director of Schroder and Co. in Los Angeles, routinely draws others into his journey. He often gives colleagues and friends books he has found compelling, thereby provoking a dialogue.

Effective leaders know that, ultimately, they are measured by their ability to influence others. In reconciling the forces of interdependence and diversity, they invite those around them to join their quest for greater meaning. By calling supporters to change the world for the better, connective leaders present constituents with elevating opportunities. They also stand as shining examples. Nelson Mandela is one such connective leader. Emerging from years of potentially embittering imprisonment, Mandela called upon South Africans of all races to forgo their animosities to strengthen a common homeland. He challenged the entire nation to build a nonracial democracy where all groups could share power and responsibility. Mandela's own great sacrifices for justice and democracy served as a model even for the skeptical.

Corporate leaders can spur their employees to make compa-
rable sacrifices for the good of the organization, the customers,
and the community. In 1996, the Pratt & Whitney aerospace
plant in North Berwick, Maine, faced closure. Robert Ponchak,
the plant manager, pushed, prodded, implored, and inspired employees to think lean, cut costs, and improve quality. Not only
did the plant escape downsizing; it also won the company's Product Center Excellence Award for three consecutive years.

In brief, connective leaders manage interdependence and
diversity by calling upon a set of special strategies. They use a
spectrum of ethical, politically savvy behaviors to integrate the
opposing forces of interdependence and diversity. Their vision
links diverse groups. They seek to connect their vision to those
of others, even when that means amending their dream. They
model authenticity and accountability. Beyond that, they search
for ennobling experiences to share with supporters. They bring
others into the leadership circle and nurture successors. Their
ability to think long-term and act short-term connects the present with the future.

Principles of
Connective Leadership

Connective leadership is based on the ordinary behaviors most
of us learned early on for achieving our goals, be they serving as
team captain, studying algebra, or designing computer software.
These behaviors may be thought of as our "achieving styles."

Over time, we tend to limit ourselves to a narrow set of
achieving styles, those with which we've experienced success.
The outcome: The broader repertoire of behaviors essential for
connective leadership—and available to everyone—atrophies.

The behavioral foundations of connective leadership can be divided into three major sets of achieving styles: the direct, relational, and instrumental sets (see figure). Within each set, there are three broad strategies with which individuals can accomplish their goals. People can and often do choose from any or, ideally, from all of these nine styles, depending on the circumstances.

People who prefer the direct set of achieving styles tend to concentrate on their own tasks. Closely linked to the forces of diversity, these styles are well suited to individual striving. Three strategies constitute the direct style of leadership:

- *Intrinsic*—deriving satisfaction, even exhilaration, from mastering one's own task, measured against an internal standard of excellence

- *Competitive*—outdoing others, measuring one's accomplishment against an external standard of performance

- *Power*—taking charge, delegating tasks, and coordinating the action of others

People who prefer to work on group tasks or to help others attain their goals draw on the relational set of leadership styles. These relational styles are analogous to the societal force of interdependence. These are the three relational styles:

- *Collaborative*—working with others on a group task, sharing both credit and responsibility for the accomplishment

- *Contributory*—playing a behind-the-scenes role or helping others complete their tasks

- *Vicarious*—taking satisfaction from facilitating, coaching, and observing the accomplishments of others

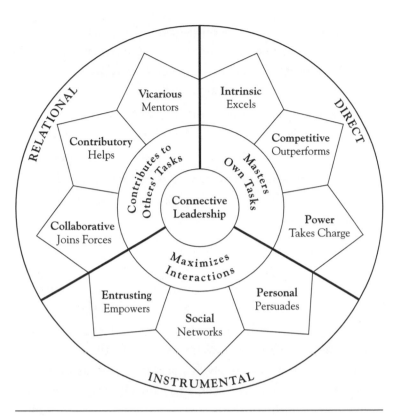

Leadership Style Sets
Source: Jean Lipman-Blumen, *The Connective Edge*, Jossey-Bass, 1996.

The *instrumental* set of leadership styles is characterized by political know-how. Most traditional models of leadership include direct and relational leadership skills, but they often ignore instrumental leadership. Connective leaders, however, use instrumental action to integrate the self-oriented and the group-oriented leadership styles. Individuals who see themselves and others as instruments for achieving their goals prefer these styles:

- *Personal*—using all of one's personal assets, including intelligence, wit, humor, charm, physical attractiveness, family background, and educational attainment to attract supporters

- *Social*—creating and employing social networks and alliances, as well as using others—and their networks and resources—to accomplish mutual goals

- *Entrusting*—relying on others to enhance a shared vision without supervision, but with strong expectations for success

Research spanning more than half a century has demonstrated that leadership is not reducible to a set of inborn traits. Most people can cultivate their particular leadership gifts. At the Drucker Graduate School of Management, studies of more than 40,000 managers have shown a great diversity of leadership styles. This research has demonstrated the effectiveness of each of these leadership styles in given situations. Still other research has traced the rewards that accrue to individuals who value and organizations that reward connective leadership. These studies make clear that learning to be a connective leader is not only possible but absolutely necessary to achieving lasting and meaningful results.

Becoming a connective leader requires serious effort. For traditional leaders, this involves understanding fresh ideas and practicing unfamiliar leadership responses. For traditional followers, it means becoming active constituents.

Although connective leadership adds the new dimension of ethical instrumentalism, it does not discard all previously learned leadership strategies. Rather, connective leadership builds on what effective leaders already know how to do. But it deepens and revitalizes the best traditional strategies, while offering new ways to be effective.

For today's leaders, the greatest danger stems from clinging to outmoded strategies. For today's constituents, the greatest danger lurks in insisting upon traditional behavior from their leaders and waiting passively for marching orders. Both strategies are sure-fire methods for missing the enormous opportunities of the future.

Connective leadership is not for the fainthearted. Not infrequently, it requires us to choose between the logic of consequences, that is, expected results, and the logic of aspirations that express our noblest identity. There are no easy problems and no easy solutions in the Connective Era.

The challenges of the Connective Era will inevitably multiply. Only those leaders with the most extensive, flexible leadership repertoires will be able to meet the dynamic demands of the Connective Era. Only those leaders with the capacity to harness the tensions spawned by interdependence and diversity will gain the connective edge.

Jean Lipman-Blumen is the Thornton F. Bradshaw Professor of Public Policy and professor of organizational behavior at the Peter F. Drucker Graduate Management School in Claremont, California. She is cofounder and codirector of the school's Institute for Advanced Studies in Leadership and an adviser to business, nonprofit, and government organizations. Her books include *Connective Leadership* and, with Hal Leavitt, *Hot Groups*.

9

Sustaining Growth: The Business of Leaders

An Interview with William C. Steere Jr.

The only acceptable business plan in today's world is growth. It is important to select organizational leaders who have the attributes and skills to deliver growth. Keys to sustaining growth are: identifying and focusing on what the organization does best; seeking growth opportunities both inside (e.g., through innovation) and outside (e.g., through partnering) the organization; creating clear performance objectives and sharing them appropriately; listening to divergent points of view and inviting debate; creating a culture of trust and autonomy; and challenging conventional wisdom.

Pfizer, Inc. has grown from a small business—founded 150 years ago in Brooklyn, New York—to a global pharmaceutical enterprise. The firm is widely recognized for its research and development breakthroughs in almost every disease category, as well as its industry-leading marketing and sales groups. Pfizer's launches, including Celebrex (arthritis), Viagra (impotence), and Lipitor (cholesterol), are among the most successful in the history of the drug industry. Its takeover of Warner-Lambert Co. makes Pfizer the largest pharmaceutical firm in the United States and the second largest in the world.

Leader to Leader asked management consultant and author Robert Shaw to speak with William Steere, chairman and CEO of Pfizer, about the challenges of leading a high-growth firm in a rapidly changing industry.

Robert Shaw: What do you see as your most important challenge?

William Steere: My primary responsibility is working with colleagues to create the strategies, culture, and capabilities needed for us to grow. This is critical because the only acceptable business plan in today's world is growth. Investors, partners, and talent all gravitate to the fastest-growing firms in any industry. High-growth firms thus create a momentum that increases the likelihood of future success.

Sustaining growth as you become larger is the real challenge—especially when you grow as we have at 20 percent a year. Wall Street can be very tough on those who fail to deliver on expectations. Some leaders, in their desire to meet aggressive growth targets, make poor strategic decisions. For example, most of the recent acquisitions in our industry occurred because a firm's product pipeline was empty. Out of weakness, they sought to cut costs. Many of these post-merger firms have sales growth of only 4 percent or 5 percent—along with 20 percent increases in earnings per share! Making your earnings by reducing your costs is a death spiral if you don't address the fundamental weaknesses that forced you to merge. You don't cut your way to long-term growth.

RS: Some are surprised by Pfizer's pursuit of a major acquisition after years of avoiding the merger and acquisition consolidation within your industry. Why the shift?

WS: This is really not a shift in our approach. We have said for years that we would not seek a merger or acquisition out of weakness. Over the years, we have avoided what we believed were poor business combinations, even when others were racing to put deals together. We are now seeking to acquire a firm that has a growth rate that matches our own and fits well with our overall strategy. We know Warner-Lambert as a result of our work together on an extremely successful partnership (marketing Lipitor). We view this as building on our mutual strengths rather than compensating for any weaknesses.

Pfizer is a highly entrepreneurial firm that evaluates each proposal on its own terms. When we saw a unique opportunity to strengthen Pfizer, we acted. We don't relish the idea of a hostile takeover. It is not our style. However, we are very deliberate once we decide on a course of action. Our personal preferences are less important than doing what is right for the company and our shareholders in creating the foundation for continued growth.

RS: What, then, do you look for in leaders who can deliver growth?

WS: I look for two potentially conflicting leadership attributes. First, you need to have a clear point of view on how to win in your industry. With this comes a great deal of faith in your own insight and ability to make the right decisions. Everyone has moments of doubt as a leader but at the core you must be extremely confident. People follow those who passionately believe in their vision for the business. The confidence of our leadership team is evident in the decisions we have made over the past decade. For example, we began to invest heavily in R&D when other firms were cutting back. We took a lot of heat from Wall Street and the press for our commitment to R&D. Our stock price suffered. As criticism mounted, I kept our board informed. We didn't ask the board to solve our problems but we reviewed our key challenges and plan of action. Working with your board to deliver long-term growth is more important than playing to Wall Street.

RS: What is the second leadership attribute needed to sustain growth?

WS: You must be able to listen to diverse points of view and not let your ego get in the way of making the right decision. My ability to listen to people is my strongest leadership capability. Remaining open to conflicting or even painful information keeps you from becoming complacent and insular. This is important because success is achieved when you have very smart people advancing different points of view on key issues. Most leaders, however, don't like tension. Some try to avoid it by creating formal hierarchies in which they make most of the decisions. Others staff their organizations with people who look and act like themselves. Many simply avoid tough issues and conflicting points of view—hoping they will go away. You don't, however, get the creative tension needed for growth if you have an organization that is too homogeneous, too hierarchical, too polite. We have a very diverse group of leaders who are rarely unanimous on any important issue. Our goal is for everyone to be heard and every point of view examined. In some cases, it is obvious what to do. In other situations, we can't agree and in the end it is my decision. But everyone knows, in these cases, that I have considered his or her perspective.

RS: Which leadership behaviors undermine a firm's ability to sustain growth?

WS: I detest arrogance. When I find it, whether in a product manager or in a research scientist, I speak out against it. That doesn't stamp it out by any means, but people understand my feelings. Overall, I see our people acting with a great deal of confidence in our vision and our abilities, without becoming arrogant. Look at what happened to some highly visible firms as they grew from small family businesses to very large corporations. Over time, many became insular and lost touch with the marketplace. Arrogance is the beginning of the end in remaining agile. Arrogant companies—and leaders—fail to see or react to new threats. They also miss opportunities to partner with others, because they want to do it all themselves. Creating a culture where people act with self-confidence without becoming arrogant is an ongoing challenge.

RS: Any knowledge-based organization relies on collaboration. How do you foster a team approach to leadership?

WS: I was a science major in college but came up through the commercial side of the company. I have an appreciation of the contributions made by people in these two different sides of our business, and the need for them to work collaboratively to deliver on our growth objectives. I also understand the operational issues in key areas of our business. However, I don't make decisions that others should make. My approach does require a very clear system of performance measures and a high level of trust. Leaders who share our values and deliver on their performance commitments have a great deal of autonomy to grow their areas of the business. I trust them until they prove that they are unworthy of it. Once I can't rely on somebody, however, they must go. In my experience, you either trust those you work with and treat them accordingly, or you can't work with them.

RS: How do you gain alignment in a dispersed, complex firm?

WS: In most of our key leadership positions, we have people who have spent decades with Pfizer. They understand how we operate and how to get things done. We strive to achieve alignment by making our objectives completely transparent. My direct reports get a copy of my annual objectives (which are approved by our board). They also get the objectives of their peers. At midyear, we look as a group at how people are doing and at the end of the year we look at performance. Transparent objectives are an important part of our performance-focused culture. In sales, for example, a publicly displayed ranking reveals how salespeople performed against their targets. You live and die by the numbers. If individuals don't make their commitments, it's pretty public. But there is no one who hasn't on occasion missed his or her numbers. In assessing shortfalls, we look at the total picture. Let's say we have a product that patients have to take three times a day and a competitor comes out with a one-a-day treatment. It's hard to be too critical when confronted with this type of situation.

RS: How do you maintain focus while trying to find new opportunities for growth?

WS: We are periodically approached by firms who want to merge with us, just as we seek out such opportunities. One interesting outcome of listening to proposals is clarifying your own thinking about what is important to you and your firm. You get a visceral feel for differences in how different companies operate when you talk with a potential merger partner. In one of these periods of reflection, I concluded that our company, all told, discovers, develops, and brings to market new medicines. That simple perspective allowed us to make significant changes in how we operate. In particular, we began to shed everything outside our primary focus (including our chemical, cosmetics, minerals, and medical device businesses). I saw these as distractions from our most important growth business. I also believe that we were not very good at running those "non-core" businesses. Over my years as CEO I have concluded that successful firms focus on what they do best. Some firms, such as GE, effectively compete in a variety of sectors—but they are the exception.

RS: How can leaders best deal with the risks associated with growth?

WS: What scares anyone leading a multinational pharmaceutical company is risk. Ours is a high-risk, high-reward business. You start with 5,000 compounds to produce one drug that makes it to the pharmacy shelf. The risk is so great that you can't exclusively manage your growth on the basis of internal innovation. We've tried to instill the notion that not all great ideas reside within Pfizer. For example, if our scientists believe a specific receptor is responsible for asthma, they will scan a variety of internal and external databases to identify opportunities. Then we will partner as needed with other firms, large and small, to bring better products to market faster. At the same time, we foster a spirit of internal innovation so that we're not overly dependent on outside intellectual property. To that end, we want to have the best R&D capability in our industry and become the partner of choice for other firms seeking to co-develop and market new pharmaceutical products. We are trying to create a culture of innovation, where we recognize and reward people based on innovative ideas, regardless of the source.

RS: Leaders today must achieve results more through informal influence than formal authority. How does this work at Pfizer?

WS: One of the toughest jobs in our company is being a product manager. Looking back on my career, this is where I personally developed my approach to team-based leadership. At Pfizer, product managers have a lot of responsibility but few if any direct reports. You may be responsible for launching a billion-dollar drug but have no staff. In other words, you are responsible for developing and implementing a plan that requires the active support of others who don't report to you. These people are often powerful in their own functions and can stop a program if they don't agree with your approach. Our most effective product managers can influence without direct control. That is a quality I look for in leaders at every level, because in today's world you don't have direct control in many situations (consider an alliance of equals). Even when you do, forcing others to comply rarely produces truly outstanding results.

RS: As a leader, how do you view the change in your industry?

WS: Change creates opportunity for agile leaders. We have to anticipate and influence some of the changes, and we have to effectively react to other changes. Change also creates more change. People say to me, "We have just divested all of our device businesses. When is all the churning and turmoil going to be over?" I tell them that it's never going to be over. We live in an industry with new competitors, constantly changing regulations, and new approaches to health care. Those who are comfortable dealing with change are the future leaders of our company. Those seeking permanence and stability, or who can work only in a clearly defined hierarchy, are out of sync with today's business challenges.

At each stage of responsibility, individuals are tested in their ability to manage change and additional complexity. Consider what happens when we take sales representatives and make them district managers. Some, by power of their intellect and personality, grow and become good district managers. You then promote the best of these individuals to regional managers (who manage managers). At each level, however, you see a larger-than-expected number of people stumble and fail. Remember that we are promoting our very best people and we expect all of them to succeed. You don't really know how someone will perform until you put him or her in a more demanding position. Even when a board picks a new CEO, everyone holds their breath and waits to see what will happen. I know they did with me. I have a very different style from my predecessor and our board—as does every board—made a decision on my promotion with incomplete information. You can pick up the *Wall Street Journal* on any day and see examples of leadership choices that didn't work out. This is particularly true now that boards are under so much pressure to play an activist role in the governance of a company.

RS: How do effective leaders learn and develop?

WS: You learn, particularly during your first few years as CEO, how to deal with the complexity of the job and develop a decision-making style that works for you and the company. I've never had a problem with decisions. There are just a lot more of them as you move up into more senior leadership positions. You also find that some decisions, no matter what path you choose, are wrong. Sometimes you have to select between two options and both are bad. Then you have to decide which is the lesser of two

---

Lessons from the Chairman

Pfizer's William Steere offers six keys to sustaining growth:

- *Focus on what you do best.* To identify opportunities, you must identify your primary strength. Concentrate on that core capability, and shed everything that distracts you from it.

- *Cast a wide net.* Seek out growth opportunities both inside and outside the firm. Promoting internal innovation is necessary but insufficient; external partners also are essential to bring better products to market, faster.

- *Create transparent objectives.* Everyone needs clear performance targets, and those targets should be shared at the appropriate level. Senior executives should review their colleagues' annual goals (and performance) twice a year.

- *Listen to divergent points of view.* While believing strongly in their view of the business, leaders must encourage other perspectives and invite rigorous debate on key issues.

- *Create a culture of trust.* To excel, people must have autonomy. Let others make their own decisions, unless they prove to be untrustworthy—in which case they must go.

- *Go with your instincts.* Effective leaders have the confidence to challenge conventional wisdom. You must be willing to withstand criticism in order to move the organization forward.

evils. You get strong people on both sides advocating one option over another. It's easier when someone else is making the call. Then, one day, I was the one making the final decisions on a variety of tough issues. Some of these decisions are obvious. Some are intuitive. Others keep you up at night.

Every senior leader learns on the job. You need to find sources of support as you learn from your successes and mistakes. When faced with difficult decisions, however, you often can't go to members of your team for "off-line" conversations because they may misinterpret your comments or look at it as an opportunity to lobby for a particular outcome. Several members of our board were very helpful to me over the years. I also relied on a former Pfizer CEO during my early years. In my case, I went back two generations of CEOs for support. Periodically, I would meet with him to discuss the critical issues I was facing. As a CEO mentor, he was probably the best help I had. He had been in my role at Pfizer, so he understood what I was up against. He also had a wonderful sense of humor that helped reinforce his points. I recall, for example, being on a plane trip with him and reading a management book on culture change. He came up to me, asked me what I was reading, took it out of my hands, and threw it away. All he said was, "You have the answers. Trust your instincts."

Before his retirement, **William C. Steere Jr.** was chairman of the board and CEO of Pfizer, Inc. He began his career with Pfizer in 1959 as a medical service representative and moved through a variety of marketing and management positions. He was elected president and chief executive officer in 1991 and chairman in 1992. During his years as CEO, Pfizer's sales doubled, net income tripled, and stock price increased eightfold.

Robert Shaw consults with senior executive teams on strategic organizational change. His most recent book is *Trust in the Balance: Building Successful Organizations on Results, Integrity, and Concern.*

10

Reinventing
Management
Development

Mark C. Maletz and Jon R. Katzenbach

Changes in today's marketplace require organizations to go beyond traditional training and development to help managers develop entrepreneurial capabilities. The authors describe how one organization conducted a program that included classroom modules; entrepreneurial fieldwork that consisted of developing real businesses; and coaching and mentoring support from academics, consultants, and industry experts.

" The most important thing we do is hire great people. I don't place much stock in management development—people really don't change much. . . . When I first started out in business, I thought I could change anyone—given the right set of circumstances. Now I realize that great people have certain intrinsic qualities (intelligence, integrity, a sense of what matters, and an ability to relate to others). . . . Those characteristics are much more important than any skill they might develop along the way."

This statement by the CEO of a successful financial services company reflects the attitude of many top executives, and helps

115

explain why many are questioning the effectiveness of their organizations' management development efforts. Top executives
have seen few tangible results from their past investments in
developing future leaders. Hence it is easier to concentrate on
hiring those who are able to develop themselves, and let them
"work it out" in the heat of battle.

The problem is, you quickly run out of talent if you rely solely
on hiring and self-development. A recent survey of corporate of-
ficers and high-potential executives from 77 leading companies
indicates that the most glaring gap in the eyes of these leaders
was "development." Few companies believe they do it well—and
most high-performing individuals expect it to be done better.

Moreover, organizations today routinely face hairpin turns
in strategic direction or radical redesign of organizational structures, and such abrupt changes usually require different capabilities than current managers have. For example, the dramatic
move of Enron—formerly a gas pipeline company—into the financial services arena was a strategic coup; SmithKline's merger
with Beecham in 1989 created a new culture of global propor-
tions; and when ABB adopted its well-publicized matrix structure including 1,200 autonomous business units, it set the stage
for companies around the world to radically disaggregate their
organizational structures. Sudden and complex changes like
these are becoming commonplace.

Organizations undergoing change must find ways to develop
new individual and institutional capabilities—not only to achieve
strategic goals, but also to attract and retain the best people. In
high-growth organizations, development opportunities are abundant. The paradox comes when sustaining growth requires skills
that managers do not possess—and cannot easily acquire exter-
nally. It is then the "development gap" begins to pinch.

"Management development" carries a lot of baggage, and is often equated with formal training. For that reason, organizations that most effectively develop their talent view the process as "capability building"—a broad-based, integrated effort that goes well beyond training and self-development.

Building Entrepreneurial Managers

One multinational high-tech company sought to develop the entrepreneurial capabilities of its general managers, applying principles that characterize the world's best management development programs. The company had just announced the creation of more than 250 profit and loss units (replacing a many-layered hierarchy where P&L responsibility resided only with the top team). The sheer magnitude of instituting this new structure was further complicated by a bureaucratic culture that smothered the responsiveness and initiative demanded by the new environment.

The first and perhaps most daunting question for the program was simply *who would manage these 250 units?* Top management could not identify even 20 managers who had the capability to step immediately into these positions. The jobs required an extraordinary combination: a general management competence to manage a P&L with $50 million to $100 million in annual revenue and between 100 and 300 employees, *and* the attitudes and experience to create an entrepreneurial approach to customers and growth. This would be a formidable task for any manager, especially a new one! The solution was to develop the needed managers through an "entrepreneurship development program"—not as simple as it sounds.

Nonetheless, the program has been remarkably successful. During 1996 and 1997, more than 400 managers attended the program. They gave it high marks but, more important, could point to real business results they achieved while building new entrepreneurial capabilities.

Why Entrepreneurship?

Senior executives were initially skeptical that entrepreneurship, rather than general management skills, was the proper focus. But the need for change and growth was compelling. The only way forward was to develop the entrepreneur's fierce competitive drive and relentless focus on customer needs. Moreover, entrepreneurs *quickly* become adept at operating in changing environments. In fact, they often work to shape environmental changes to their advantage, and are obsessed in their pursuit of growth.

The pure entrepreneur seldom survives in a large organization. Such individuals are driven to create their own enterprises, wherein personal fortunes can be made—and personal net worth is at stake. Of course, outside of start-up companies, such dramatic financial incentives are rare. However, companies can promote greater entrepreneurship by combining sound managerial practices with entrepreneurial behavior and by crafting variable pay or bonus systems that give managers a significant stake in their success. To develop its entrepreneurial capability, this large company focused on three key attributes.

- An action orientation:
  Ability to deliver results
  Willingness to take and manage risk
  Innovation and creativity
- General management skills:
  Focus on the customer

Team and networking capability
Business analysis

- Leadership and influence:
Capacity to set direction and coach for success
Ability to learn (from successes and failures)
Balance of "big picture" with operational activities

These critical skills became the core of an entrepreneurship development program.

Entrepreneurial Learning Process

Participants learned how to network with one another and with other key managers in the company, both to share experiences on an ongoing basis and to collaborate in the market. Participants continued to meet and collaborate long after they "graduated" from the program. Moreover, many graduates went on to mentor others in the company and in the process tested their entrepreneurial leadership. Finally, participants received coaching from recognized experts inside and outside the company. This coaching was instrumental in their mastery of the new management skills and entrepreneurial behaviors.

The program was organized around what became known as the entrepreneurship life cycle of *creating, developing, and implementing opportunities*. Each of these one- to two-week classroom modules was separated by one to three months of fieldwork during which participants could apply what they had learned in the classroom. In effect, this process served as an R&D lab for entrepreneurial opportunities within participants' business units—an Internet services offering, a network security product, a new retail channel for low-cost products, or creation of a new sales group to focus on universities and research centers. Every member of the company's executive board attended at least one half-day of the program for each wave of participants. The CEO often spent two days with each wave.

The key to the fieldwork was putting classroom concepts into practice—and then combining them with coaching support from a "virtual faculty" of outsiders (academics, consultants, industry experts) and insiders (senior managers, functional experts, mentors, graduates of previous programs). The fieldwork was central to the business objectives of the participants. In this way, the program design helped participants work more effectively, rather than being an onerous source of "additional work to do."

More than 80 percent of the participants fully implemented their entrepreneurial opportunities, enabling the company to fill the open P&L unit manager positions and maintain a strong managerial bench for new units. Of course, participants were screened carefully and understood how important it was to succeed with all eyes upon them. More than a dozen new units were conceived and launched by program graduates. By the last wave of the program, participants had generated almost a half-billion dollars of incremental revenue.

The biggest win of the program was a new business selling automated "point of sale" gas pumps to European oil companies. The leader of this effort had no previous general management—nor oil industry—experience. By graduation, though, he had signed a deal worth more than $100 million dollars over 10 years and was negotiating several other deals.

Even the more typical successes were impressive. Consider the 28-year-old participant who created a niche business in Scandinavia selling telecommuting solutions to companies who wanted to let employees work from home. This manager had visited the

United States on vacation and, on the flight from Europe, had talked to a U.S.-based consultant who worked from home. The participant then spent half of his vacation looking into telecommuting in the United States. The business he launched on his return generated $2.2 million in its first year of operation. Every such financial success was supported by new learning and behavior that extended the success beyond the project at hand.

Principles for Success

While capability building can address any needed skills (particularly those linked to an organization's strategic priorities), it can be broadly applied to leadership and operational excellence. The effort requires patience, mentoring, both on-the-job and classroom learning, and consistent line management support. It also requires persistence, innovation, and a willingness to reflect and learn from successes and failures. Because it works in theory *and* practice, at both the individual and institutional level, capability building is far more dynamic than the passive notion of training.

Effective capability-building efforts encompass 10 operational principles (see "Principles of Capability Building").

But two fundamentals underlie any capability building effort:

• *Capability building is based on current adult learning theory.* Adults learn when it matters to them and when they understand why they succeeded or failed. They learn through experience and from their peers, with multiple iterations and just-in-time tools and support.

For example, a lecture about the entrepreneurial life cycle might be combined with visits to start-ups, venture capitalists, and research labs, thereby allowing participants to observe this

---

Principles of
Capability Building

- Focus on skills that can be developed, rather than traits or intrinsic personal attributes.

- Identify specific communities within the organization that are critical to achieving results.

- Consider several elements of development including training, mentoring, coaching, and special assignments.

- Ensure that top management regards the issue as a priority and will be directly involved.

- Use high-impact projects to ground the concepts and tools in the real world.

- Integrate capability building with other important strategic initiatives.

- Make capability building an ongoing part of the overall management process.

- Provide program participants with adequate time for reflection, individually and with one another.

- Ensure that participants share what they learn with others in the organization.

- Monitor capability-building efforts and ensure clarity of progress and results.

---

life cycle firsthand. To further enrich the learning, participants might also socialize at local hang-outs with people from these start-ups—with affable interchange underscoring learning and opening further avenues for it.

• *Capability building pays for itself.* The best approaches result in a kind of "earn as you learn" model crafted around strategically significant business projects. Such efforts simultaneously develop required capabilities *and* deliver performance impact. Participants must bring real work to the program—often in the form of strategic initiatives that are sponsored by senior managers; leaders can achieve similar results by organizing learning around any critical performance issue. The "application" for joining one leadership development program is a proposal for an important strategic initiative. There are no "toy projects" or hypothetical issues in programs that build true strategic capabilities. The participant is always expected to implement what is learned.

Typical management training fails because the lessons are not easily transferred back into the reality of everyday work. It is not that participants have a hard time learning or are uninterested—usually the reverse is true. The problem is that those who lead training programs often fail to understand the particular challenges and opportunities faced by the students.

Capability building should be organized around natural "communities" (work groups that share common values and objectives and that interact with one another on a regular basis). Organizing around natural communities helps ensure that the program delivers tangible results and that members continue to share experiences long after the formal elements of the program have been completed. After all, much of the pleasure of executive activity comes from working within a cadre of talented and trusted colleagues who learn from one another.

Finally, capability building is most powerful when delivered by a mix of outsiders and insiders who together provide relevant subject expertise, a realistic understanding of the company, and just-in-time coaching. One of the most common and serious weaknesses of executive education programs is poor integration across the faculty. While individual lectures may be interesting, they are often difficult for participants to synthesize. Worse, they are disconnected from business realities.

Succeeding at Capability Building

Despite the results possible from capability development, six challenges face an organization pursuing such an approach.

• Changing the ways in which people think and behave is hard; "unlearning" is often even more difficult than learning.

• Designing experiences that support self-discovery requires fresh thinking. In one program designed to develop change leadership in a major industrial company, participants visited one of the world's foremost teaching hospitals. They interviewed managers coping with America's health care crisis, and "consulted" to the hospital. Although health care and industrial sectors are very different, both must deal with an environment of rapid change. By looking at health care, the participants could focus on the impact of this environmental change and avoid getting lost in the details.

• Coaches themselves must be coached. Effective coaching is often characterized as an art form. However, it is a capability that can be learned by many people. Coaches have to know, for instance, when to provide support and when to let participants learn by doing (even if this means experiencing some failure).

• Since acquiring new capabilities can be risky and uncomfortable, capability building requires the construction of "safe envelopes" in which new behaviors and skills can be practiced.

It is, however, important to balance these safe envelopes with the need for real work. New capabilities can be practiced in the classroom but must, ultimately, be mastered in the field.

• The very experiences that shape the learning can overtake it. For example, participants working to lead a change project might become so focused on succeeding at the immediate task that they fail to reflect on the broader learning opportunities presented by the project.

• Participants in capability-building programs must be master jugglers: they have to experience new ways of working while remaining connected to the old ways still present in the workplace. If they don't, they may be ineffective at transferring the new capabilities to others.

Organizations that meet these challenges simultaneously build new capabilities and deliver performance impact for the business. The challenge of identifying and integrating effective learning experiences is significant. It goes well beyond even the best of training programs today, and taps all aspects of the work environment as well as relevant external knowledge sources. Clearly it is a serious investment of both financial and human resources. However, the benefits will greatly exceed the investment costs—and for most organizations it will be a fundamental matter of survival.

Mark C. Maletz is a principal in McKinsey & Company's Organization Practice and associate professor of management at Babson College. He has been responsible for more than 50 large-scale change initiatives across a variety of industries, focusing on the strategy, structure, and culture of the changing organizations.

Jon R. Katzenbach is founding and senior partner of Katzenbach Partners LLC, consultants in the areas of team, leadership, and workforce performance. He was a director at McKinsey & Co. for 39 years. He is author, coauthor, or editor of six books including *The Wisdom of Teams*, and, most recently, *The Discipline of Teams*.

11

The New Age
of Persuasion

Jay Conger

*As organizational control shifts away from traditional hier-
archy, managers and leaders need to have the power of persuasion in order to influence others. A major aspect of this is
the ability to understand the expectations, concerns, and feelings of the hearers and to frame communication to connect
with their interests—to describe goals and rewards that satisfy mutual interests. By emphasizing the positive future while
highlighting current dangers, leaders can mobilize action.*

A historic shift is taking place in the nature of leading. The
tradition of leading by the power of one's position is being
challenged by a new model shaped by intense competition, cross-
functional teamwork, new workplace generations, and the networked organization. Global competition is forcing organizations
to respond far more quickly to their marketplaces, and more and
more of the work of organizations is accomplished by independent contractors, outside partners, and professionals over whom
leaders have little formal authority.

This new reality is challenging the traditional command-
and-control organization, whose upward delegation of decisions
slows reaction time and increases costs without adding value.

It is shifting decision-making power to people in the middle and periphery of the organization who have growing discretion in how to best solve problems, serve customers, and respond to opportunities.

Other trends—especially the spreading impact of electronic communication—are accelerating the erosion of traditional authority. All of these forces underscore a new reality for today's leaders: our most important asset is the ability to use language persuasively. In a world where leading is no longer accomplished by edict, much of the leader's day is necessarily spent persuading colleagues in meetings and hallway chats to accept proposed solutions for business problems.

Forces for Change

Three forces in particular are changing the requirements for effective leadership.

- *The cross-functional team.* When you watch effective cross-functional teams, you quickly realize why we use them. They are information-generating machines. In a single setting, they can maximize the number of perspectives and solutions on a given issue. From this rich pool of information, sounder and better coordinated initiatives flow naturally. They also are fast. Companies have halved the time it takes to go from an initial product design to finished product—simply by employing cross-functional teams. This team approach, however, challenges the traditions of power and authority. For example, while there is normally an appointed leader, few if any members of the team have formal reporting relationships to one another. Certain functions may indeed have greater status, but the use of authority in cross-functional teams dampens the very output they are seeking—the free flow of information and debate.

The well-designed team runs like a collective of peers rather than a group of bosses and subordinates. But the question naturally arises, "How do you influence your peers?" Certainly not through formal orders. Your expertise is one source. But remember, the team came together because no one person had all the answers. The strength of the relationships around the table is another source. But in the end, the ability to persuade will more effectively guarantee that each of us will be heard and, more important, that our ideas and solutions will contribute to the team's outcomes.

• *Changing workplace generations.* Baby boomers are today's senior executives, while Generation Xers are typically front-line managers. In contrast to their predecessors, both these generations tend to be suspicious of those in power. After all, the Boomers watched a failed war in Vietnam, disgraced presidents, environmental disasters, the OPEC oil crisis, and a series of assassinations. These events fostered a basic distrust of authority—it was not only unreliable but often plain wrong.

But a larger part of these generations' attitudes toward authority were shaped by their parents' beliefs. Both the Boomers and Generation X have been raised to be independent thinkers. In surveys covering more than a century, only 16 percent of parents in 1890 believed that independence was an important attribute for their children, while 64 percent ranked obedience as highly important. But by the end of the 1970s, those numbers had nearly reversed. Approximately 75 percent of all parents felt that independence was the most important character trait; obedience was considered important by only 17 percent of parents. These, of course, are the parents of Generation X.

Furthermore, both generations were the beneficiaries of the greatest surge in education in history. The percentage of men and women graduating from college has more than doubled since

1960. Sitting in classrooms throughout America, they found themselves encouraged to critique the ideas and books they were studying. They were taught to challenge one another's thinking and even the professor's, not to blindly accept received wisdom. As a result, they are best led through convincing arguments rather than commands. A 40-something senior manager of a global bank—normally a traditional command-and-control environment—nicely sums it up: "You have to continually show [people] what it is they're getting out of this organization. Continually you have to make it a two-way street. That's the way you get their commitment. Commanding these generations won't do much to motivate them. They've got to be informed and convinced and informed again. If you want their commitment, you've got to persuade them."

• *The electronic erosion of authority.* The final force eroding the old command model sits on your desk peering straight at you—the computer. By giving knowledge workers access to information from throughout the organization and around the world, this technology is breaking hierarchical norms. As futurist Alvin Toffler has commented, a junior manager can now directly communicate with senior executives working on the same problem. Executives, in turn, can jump many levels below to examine a spreadsheet or explore ideas for a new product with any member of their organization. Technology is creating new doorways to ensure that ideas are heard from all levels. But having our ideas heard is quite different from having them accepted. This latter step depends upon our ability to persuade others of their value. In a freer and broader electronic marketplace of ideas, it will be the managers who are most adept at convincing others who will be heard.

When subordinates have access to the same information as their bosses, they can assess the boss's ideas more critically—

and are less likely to accept an order without first asking why. Bosses will find themselves having to be far more persuasive in explaining why their initiatives and visions of the future are the most appropriate.

Increasingly, the pathway to leading will be through well-crafted persuasion and compelling language, not formal orders. As AlliedSignal CEO Lawrence Bossidy said, "The day when you could yell and scream and beat people into good performance is over. Today you have to appeal to them by helping them see how they can get from here to there, by establishing some credibility, and by giving them some reason and some help to get there. Do all those things, and they'll knock down doors." In essence, he is describing the new language of leadership.

The Art of Framing

At the heart of successful persuasion is the notion of *framing*. Quite simply, if what you are proposing doesn't connect with the interests of your colleagues, your message will fall on deaf ears. It is crucial to understand what our audience is expecting, what they are concerned about, and what their feelings are on the issue we are addressing. As persuaders, we must never assume that our colleagues understand the advantage or necessity or urgency of what we are advocating.

How we describe or frame the purpose and intended outcomes of our thinking is critical. It tells our audience whether there is a set of mutual interests and shared beliefs on which to act. Only in this way will we get their attention and agreement. To persuade meaningfully, we must not only listen to others and understand their point of view, we must incorporate their perspectives and ideas into our positions. And we must do so in a manner that allows colleagues to feel that we have positively responded to their needs. What many managers do, in contrast, is to argue from their own viewpoint. They see the benefits so clearly; surely, they think, the person to whom they are talking can see them in the same light. This is rarely the case.

Framing is like photography. Our own perspective is one angle on a particular scene. Colleagues may prefer that we zoom in on certain details or take a wide-angle view of the issue. Our goal is to focus the lens so that the view appeals both to our audience and to ourselves. To be successful, our position needs to be based on goals and rewards that our colleagues feel are meaningful for them. In addition, a successful frame usually incorporates the values and beliefs held by an audience.

What Works, What Doesn't

A manager of the process-engineering group of an aircraft turbine manufacturer learned the importance of crafting goals with the needs of constituents in mind. He and his team had been working on various redesigns of work flow for engine maintenance. Normally, a single group might work on a DC-10 engine one week and a 727 the next. The manager and his team designed a system in which each work group specialized in one type of engine. It would require initial funding, but his plan would save significant time and money in the long run. He had to win the approval of the company's president, however, before moving ahead.

A friend on the senior team advised him to show how his new system would improve short-term profitability rather than long-term efficiency. The manager redesigned his project so it would require no capital investment, and bottom line results would show in its first year. The president enthusiastically signed off.

Unfortunately, the manager forgot to reframe the goals for the middle managers who would be called upon to implement the project. He assumed that with the president's approval, it would be accepted without question. Instead, the middle managers undermined the initiative. Had the manager considered how to frame the project's benefits to the other contributors, he would most likely have needed to make a few alterations in his plan—but these would have secured the support he needed instead of the resistance he received.

By contrast, Monica Ruffo, an account executive at a Canadian advertising agency, understood the importance of framing in a difficult leadership situation. Her client, a fast food restaurant chain, was instituting a "value meal campaign"; certain menu items were to be bundled together and sold under a single promotional price as part of a new pricing strategy. Corporate headquarters wanted to address customer perceptions that its products were overpriced. The franchisees, on the other hand, were far more concerned about the short-term impact on their profit margins.

Ruffo, who was asked to present the new strategy to the annual franchisees' meeting, rightly sensed that it would be a mistake to frame the issue from the perspective of headquarters. Instead she focused on the topic of greatest concern for the franchisees—their stores' profitability. She described a test market in Tennessee, where value pricing helped boost total sales of french fries and drinks—the two most profitable items on the menu. Her next argument was that the company had already rolled out medium-sized meal packages in 80 percent of its U.S. outlets, and that associated sales of fries and drinks had jumped 26 percent. Finally, Ruffo cited research showing that when customers raise their estimate of the value they receive by 10 percent, the establishment's sales rise by 1 percent. She estimated that the new meal plan would increase value perceptions by 100 percent and that franchisee sales could be expected to grow by some 10 percent.

Ruffo closed her presentation with a letter to the organization written years before by the company's founder. It was an emotional message extolling the values of the company and stressing the importance of the franchisees to the company's success. It also highlighted the importance of the company's positioning as the low-price leader in the industry. The beliefs and values contained in the letter had long been etched in the minds of the audience. Hearing them once again confirmed for them the company's concern for their success and the power of its winning formula (and earned Ruffo a standing ovation). Later that day, the franchisees voted unanimously to support the company's new pricing plan.

In this case, Ruffo framed the value meal initiative around the role it would play in enhancing franchisee profits. She addressed head-on the issue foremost in the minds of her audience. Had she chosen to frame the new pricing scheme as a mandate from corporate or as a vehicle simply to change consumer perceptions, she would have failed to win her audience's support.

How Leaders Mobilize Action

One of the greatest challenges facing today's leaders is the need to move their organizations boldly in new directions. It is here that framing can play a vital role. Having studied many leaders who were successful change agents, I repeatedly observed a pattern in how they described their organization's present situation and proposed direction. Cleverly, they were able to use framing to garner commitment to the future. Through frames of sharp contrast, the leader constructs images that emphasize the positive features of the future while simultaneously highlighting the dangers of the current environment. The aim is to depict the status quo as so unattractive or threatening that it creates disenchantment. This portrayal unfreezes attachments to the current situation and in turn lowers resistance to the changes the leader is advocating.

Charlotte Beers, former chairman of the advertising firm Ogilvy & Mather, has been highly effective in this approach—powerfully interpreting the status quo of her company as dire, and using her powers of framing to help propel a turnaround of the company. Upon her arrival from outside Ogilvy & Mather, Beers spent her initial months at the firm studying how the organization's services had deteriorated. After extensive fact-finding visits with clients, she shared what she had heard with Ogilvy & Mather management in a series of meetings. She revealed that clients rated the firm below other agencies. She described how clients viewed O&M staff as uninvolved, distant, and reserved and how the different departments—creative, account, media, and research—were seen to work as separate entities. She pointed to an alarming exodus of top talent.

Through these meetings, she dramatically raised awareness that the firm was failing customers—in essence, highlighting the intolerable state of the status quo and implying that the firm's future was in serious jeopardy. At the same time, she portrayed the future of Ogilvy & Mather as a great opportunity. She framed the future vision not only as a restoration of the firm's former greatness but also as a move into a new era of advertising in which Ogilvy & Mather would be the industry leader.

Her vision was justified. The firm has regained its preeminence, thanks largely to her "brand stewardship" approach to advertising. O&M has won back some of the industry's most coveted accounts and seen billings grow to $7.6 billion, a nearly 40 percent increase in five years.

Learning to Frame

At the heart of framing is a solid understanding of your audience. Before attempting to persuade, the most effective leaders study the issues that matter to their colleagues. In brief office chats or in telephone conversations or in meetings, they collect essential information. They seek out sources who are knowledgeable about their audience's concerns and hopes. They are good at listening. They test their ideas with trusted confidants, and they ask questions of the people they will later be persuading. These explorations help them think through the arguments, the evidence, and the perspectives they will present. Often, this process causes them to alter or rethink their own plans before presenting them and helps ensure ultimate acceptance. It is through this thoughtful, inquisitive approach that they develop frames and solutions that work.

The first step in the framing process is to build your position around goals and rewards shared by your audience. Start by asking yourself the following types of questions:

What aspects of my idea or proposition will have significant appeal to colleagues?

What might be attractive advantages?

How can I demonstrate these in terms of outcomes and rewards that will be meaningful to others?

If shared rewards and advantages are not apparent, how might I adapt my ideas or solutions so that these will emerge?

In short, tie your initiative to tangible benefits for all involved. That may sound like classic sales psychology, but to move skeptical constituents to action takes more than smart sales tactics. It takes demonstrated concern and genuine understanding. For example, in trying to persuade your company's chief financial officer to invest in a costly piece of equipment, you might detail the advantages it could offer the finance department in terms of more accurate costing information or reduced waste.

Step two is to incorporate values and beliefs that are regarded as important by your colleagues. Their presence adds strength to the appeal. Lee Iacocca was a master of this approach in his now famous turnaround of Chrysler. For example, in his appeal to Congress for a government bailout, he used American values of entrepreneurship and free enterprise. He talked about Chrysler as an amalgam of "little guys"—some 11,000 suppliers and 4,000 dealers. He explained that almost all were small businessmen. He focused not on the big corporation but on those who supported it—American entrepreneurs. He also described how thousands of jobs would be lost to Japanese automakers—appealing to American patriotism.

Though you will most likely not find yourself in such a massive turnaround challenge, there are nonetheless important values and beliefs behind every compelling initiative that cement commitment to their realization.

The third and final leg of framing is to pay careful attention to your language. It further reinforces the notion of a common ground with colleagues. It is important therefore to ask yourself such questions as

Does the vocabulary I have chosen match that of my listeners?

Will the tone I choose sound right to them, for this occasion?

Is the emotional level right: enthusiastic versus anxious versus confident?

Are the analogies, metaphors, and stories that I am using familiar enough that they will connect with the audience's own experiences? (See "Making a Connection to Make a Point.")

Making a Connection to Make a Point

Among the most useful tools of language are metaphors and analogies. They can be used to make a point more vivid and to capture in feelings the points we are attempting to make in our words. These qualities of vividness are particularly important in persuading others.

Research shows that most people treat statistical summaries as largely uninformative. The numbers are too abstract and colorless to be memorable. What this research suggests is that information is absorbed by listeners in proportion to its vividness. For example, Karen Fries, a product development manager at Microsoft, employed an effective and vivid analogy when persuading the company of the need for a new, highly user-friendly version of its software. This is what she said:

"Imagine you want to cook a dinner and that you must first go to the supermarket. There's all the flexibility you want—you can cook anything in the world as long as you know how, and you have the time and desire to do it. . . . You find all these overstuffed aisles with cryptic single-word headings like sundries and ethnic food and condiments. These are the menus on our computer interfaces. . . . Now after you have hunted and collected everything, you still need to put it all together in the correct order to make a meal. If you are a good cook, you will probably get a good meal. If you're a novice, probably not. We [at Microsoft] have been selling under the supermarket category for years, and we think there is a big opportunity for restaurants. If you want a good meal in a relaxing ambiance, restaurants are the ticket. That's what we are trying to do now. . . . You sit down, you get comfortable. We bring you a menu. The meal is organized around categories. . . . You simply tell us [what] you want. . . . No walking around lost trying to find things, no cooking."

Fries uses an everyday experience to convey the needs of customers. She has found an analogy that powerfully parallels problems that everyone faces. We all know the frustration of searching up and down supermarket aisles—which Fries links to the frustration of searching for functions and tools on our computers—versus the ease and pleasure of dining at a restaurant.

Her metaphor conveys connotations of enjoyment, which listeners unconsciously transfer to her proposal for more user-friendly software. Had she used a literal description of the software's features, few if any of her highly computer-literate colleagues would have appreciated the customers' frustration with their product. Instead, her vivid imagery elicited an emotional response—and that is usually what it takes to persuade others to embrace a new idea.

Our aim is to connect with our listeners rather than distance ourselves from them, for it is in the connections that real leadership develops. Effective leaders—like all good marketers and adept partners—have always understood that they must start by learning what matters to their customers, constituents, or collaborators. Faced with organizations undergoing phenomenal rates of change, managers at all levels must today do the same. We must find solutions that address the needs of others, and articulate meaningful goals and visions to carry the organization forward. After all, it is through our words that we convey meaning—meaning that can motivate our colleagues and our organizations to willingly embrace the new courses of action that our times demand.

Jay Conger is senior research scientist at the Center for Effective Organizations at the University of Southern California's Marshall School of Business. He also has taught at Harvard Business School, INSEAD, and McGill University. An authority on leadership development, board governance, and organizational change, Conger is author of more than 60 articles and 9 books, including *Winning 'Em Over*.

12

How to Lower the Risk in CEO Succession

Ram Charan

Leadership succession can be improved. First, start with the requirements for the job rather than with the candidates. Reassess the organization's current status and future direction and identify its specific needs, relevant to these considerations. Second, broaden the field by looking at candidates from inside and outside the organization. Third, evaluate the candidates as total people. Look for business acumen— the ability to consider complex relationships and changing conditions and execute the most critical operating priorities. Conduct in-depth discussions with each candidate and try to ascertain the person's past performance, personality traits, strengths, and weaknesses.

Ever since the board of General Motors ousted CEO Robert Stempel in 1992, boards of directors have been more willing to act when a CEO falters. The demands on CEOs are ever increasing, and with the pace of change accelerating, errors in strategy or execution are more frequent and more visible. Impatient investors demand action when a sustained, deep drop in stock price goes unaddressed by management. Thus a growing number of boards find themselves having to choose a new CEO—often with little firsthand experience, increasingly in the midst of company turmoil, and sometimes on the heels of a previous bad hire.

Xerox forced out Richard Thoman just 13 months after making him CEO. Apple Computer went through three CEOs in quick succession before Steve Jobs returned to set the company straight. Coca-Cola, Philip Morris, and Toys R Us have had to fill their CEO slots twice in less than three years. Mattel's Jill Barad held the top job for just two years before investors made their lack of confidence crystal clear.

Those who must select a new CEO—namely, the search committee of the board (the outgoing CEO, if he or she is in good standing, and three to five board members, most of whom should be active CEOs)—know what's at stake. Selecting the wrong person does damage to investors, employees, and the organization as a whole. In the worst case, it can cause a depletion of talent at the top and serious loss of credibility on Wall Street or among other important constituents.

In today's world, there are no sure bets. But despite the inherent risks, CEOs and directors can improve the chances that the next CEO will succeed. A few simple guidelines can help ensure a good choice and a smooth transition: first, specify the company's most crucial needs, second, broaden the field, and third, evaluate the candidates as total people. These recommendations are based on experience mostly with large corporations but apply to business or nonprofit organizations of any size.

Define What You Need

Many CEO searches are doomed before they begin for one simple reason: they start with people rather than with the requirements for the job. Some CEOs have a candidate in mind to succeed them. They may have invested years grooming the person through job rotations, coaching, and exposure to the board. When succession planning begins in earnest, they quickly jump to the specifics of handing over the baton. Board members, too, tend to fix on a handful of people, typically people they've known for years inside the organization.

Especially when the inside candidates have been successful and are well liked, succession seems automatic. But succession is an opportunity to reassess the company's overall position and future direction. The board should take a broad and forward-looking view of the business landscape and the company's emerging needs.

This job cannot be delegated. Thorough discussion of the company's needs will create a different set of criteria from the laundry list offered up by even the most respected executive recruiters. Some criteria will always appear, of course. Every company needs a CEO with high integrity and the ability to communicate and motivate people, for instance, and a CEO must not only meet the current criteria but also show an ability to grow into the job and adapt as the environment changes. Business acumen is also becoming a prerequisite for CEOs of for-profit organizations (see "The First Criterion").

However, other leadership skills that can make or break an organization are unique to the business. Every company's situation is different, and therefore the criteria for its CEO should be identified each time the succession question comes up. Does the company have a great strategy that needs to be executed? Is it at risk of being overtaken by nontraditional competitors? Is the industry converging, diverging, or consolidating?

For example, one large manufacturing company had been deriving nearly all its revenues from the United States but found

---

The First Criterion:
Business Acumen

Regardless of size, industry, or culture, the fundamentals of every business—profit margin, capital intensity, cash flow, growth, market share, and customers—are the same. Any business that can generate cash, have a positive return on assets, grow its sales and profits, build brands, and develop positive customer relationships in the face of changing conditions will achieve its long-term goals.

Understanding the elements of business success is simple. But understanding how they relate to each other, how they can be combined, and how they fit the changing environment is complex. It requires *business acumen*—the ability to cut through the complexity of relationships, variations, and changing conditions to identify and execute the operating priorities most critical to the business's ongoing profitability.

Although business acumen may seem like an obvious requirement, only recently have search committees begun to discuss it explicitly. Like many leadership abilities, business acumen can be developed and honed. But, unlike conventional definitions of leadership, it refers to how effectively one links actions to specific business results. Those with exceptional business acumen are able to diagnose and manage more than one kind of business despite immense complexity, as Jack Welch did at GE and Lou Gerstner has done at American Express, RJR Nabisco, and, finally, IBM.

---

demand slowing in its domestic market. Globalization was key to continued growth and shareholder value creation. Therefore, the search committee specified that the new CEO should have "significant international experience that will enable him or her to capitalize on global opportunities and/or reduce risk accordingly." This criterion was non-negotiable; any serious candidate had to have a demonstrated record of globalizing a company.

Another company had delivered below-expected earnings for several quarters, despite repeated reassurances that better returns were just around the corner. Wall Street analysts had begun to question the viability of the strategy (which was in fact sound) and whether the company had the wherewithal to pull out of its slump. The search committee realized that the new CEO would have to be perceived as a person who delivered on promises and could communicate effectively with investors. There was little time for learning. It specified that the new CEO should have "a reputation for managerial excellence with Wall Street, or who could be expected to swiftly build a reputation for managerial excellence with the Street."

One company was losing a CEO who had crafted a program to continually drive down costs. Changes inside the company had been hard won, and now employees and investors were gaining enthusiasm as results were beginning to materialize. The board wanted to see the momentum continue, so it specified that the new CEO should have "a sufficiently flexible management style to continue to build on key strategies that have largely driven success to date, specifically, low-cost sourcing and global logistics."

When the criteria for a CEO look like that of any other company, the people who are conducting the search have not worked hard enough to pinpoint the skills or traits critical to the organization's near-term success. When the criteria are specific and unique to the business needs at the time, they will provide useful clues about where to direct the search—inside or outside the company—and eventually, about which individual to choose.

Look Inside and Out

Directors and outgoing CEOs often assume that hiring an inside candidate will lower the risk. They feel more comfortable
going with a known quantity. Although knowing the candidate
well is an advantage, the search committee should always compare insiders and outsiders—if only to boost their confidence in
the final decision. One large telephone company had a strong
internal candidate but also identified a strong outside candidate
from a large technology company. After rigorous interviewing
and comparison, the search committee ultimately selected the
insider. That decision turned out to be a good one—the outsider flopped in two other companies and the internal candidate did a superb job.

Anxiety about going outside is understandable. Recruiting a
CEO from another company does indeed have its risks. Even
with a stellar reputation, how the chosen candidate will fit in a
new organization is always a question. And bringing someone in
from outside can be quite costly. Companies that are viewed as
good sources of talent work hard to retain their up-and-coming
leaders, and generous compensation is part of the allure. A 45-
year-old business unit manager in one large, well-respected company had a compensation package of roughly $1.25 million base
pay with up to 100 percent bonus, $25 million in restricted
stock, another $25 million available when he retires at age 65,
plus stock options.

Often, however, risk notwithstanding, boards and incumbent
CEOs have no choice but to look outside for leadership talent.
If, for instance, the organization is small and therefore has few
internal candidates (and little opportunity to test them), it will
have to recruit an outsider. Likewise, if the heir apparent is hired

away at the eleventh hour or suddenly reveals a fatal flaw, the search committee may have to look elsewhere. Both Merck and Praxair lost their top succession candidates late in the game. Some large organizations will have to look outside because of earlier cost-cutting efforts that eliminated executive develop-ment programs, reduced many senior-level jobs, and drove some high-potential leaders to seek greener pastures.

Sometimes an outsider is simply the best person for the job. (See "Insider or Outsider?") Despite a company's efforts to groom a successor, the inside candidate does not always possess the skills, experience, or perspective the company needs at the time, perhaps because those needs have changed. Xerox, IBM, and Hewlett-Packard all had succession programs that were admired and benchmarked by others, yet when it was time to appoint a new CEO, they had to go outside to find a leader with the par-ticular strengths called for at the time. Sometimes the organiza-tion needs a leader who is psychologically removed from past practices, which almost always means an outsider.

Thus inside candidates are not risk free. When the person's qualifications do not meet the key criteria, an insider can put the entire organization at risk. Besides, no one can be certain that a CEO will succeed until he or she is actually in the job. And being an insider can be a drawback when dramatic change is required.

Is it possible to combine the best of both worlds—the famil-iarity of an insider with the fresh perspective and psychological distance of an outsider? Sometimes, depending on how you de-fine "insider" and "outsider." In some older, established industries, such as automotive parts, an experienced manager within the in-dustry, not just within the organization itself, may be seen as an insider. On the other hand, an employee on the periphery of a

Insider or Outsider?

One of the first and most difficult questions in a search for a new senior executive is whether to look inside or outside the organization. An insider is best when

- The organization is on a good trajectory. No radical changes are required in the company's direction, organization, or people.

  An outsider is best when

- The business portfolio requires transformation. An insider, particularly someone from the operating side, is less likely to have the necessary skills in deal making and negotiation.

- The company must make a dramatic shift in strategy to adjust to a discontinuity, such as e-commerce. An insider will have a harder time breaking away from business as usual and may lack experience in the new arena.

- The organization must adjust to industry consolidation or the convergence of several industries. An insider will have a harder time adopting a highly objective frame of mind. An outsider is more likely to be able to reinvent and reposition the business.

- The company lacks credibility with investors. A marquee name may be needed to allay concerns about company performance. An insider would most likely be viewed as a continuation of the previous regime.

- The internal workings of the company require wholesale change. An insider, with long-term relationships and psychological bonds, will not have as much freedom to break from the past.

- The company must make a major shift, such as going from a domestic to a global business. Experience is key. It is best to look for someone who has led another company through such a shift.

very large organization may have the psychological distance of an outsider. Jack Welch, for example, had worked at General Electric for many years before becoming CEO, but he was in the plastics business, which was not one of the company's main lines.

Evaluate the Total Person

How do search committees know when they've found who they're looking for? Evaluating CEO candidates requires a great deal of information on the person's achievements and experiences—and more important, an understanding of the candidate as a total person. There is no such thing as a perfect human being, and little chance that the search committee will find someone who meets every criterion they've specified.

The important questions are, Does this person meet the most important criteria? How has this person demonstrated the ability to deliver what is promised? What are this person's blind sides? Job histories and glowing but superficial recommendations do not provide a well-rounded view of the candidate.

Despite the good intentions and personal accomplishments of search committee members, a surprising number fall victim to several common pitfalls in evaluating CEO candidates: (1) they tend to go easy on candidates, (2) they defer to headhunters (particularly when evaluating outside candidates), and (3) they succumb to the "halo effect"—the tendency to think that any executive from a "good" company is CEO material. Because companies like GE, AlliedSignal (now Honeywell), Textron, and Emerson Electric have a way of developing business-minded leaders, their executives are often courted by headhunters. Board members sometimes say things like, "Let's get someone from GE or Emerson because those people know how to make money." Although such companies are good sources of leadership talent (just as some older, entrenched companies should be avoided), every individual requires scrutiny.

Evaluating insiders is relatively easy, but familiarity can be deceptive. Chances are directors have seen the person in a variety of settings—on social occasions, making board presentations, and so on. But their knowledge of the candidate may be incomplete. Search committee members must reflect on whether they have a total picture of the individual, and they should thoroughly discuss the candidate to test whether their impressions of the person are correct.

Evaluating outsiders is more challenging but not impossible. Reference checking is paramount. The search committee must tap the headhunters' knowledge of the candidate without depending too heavily on that one source of information. Young directors, in particular, should not be intimidated by big-name headhunters. Ask the headhunter to give a full picture of the person, including personality traits and potential shortcomings. Most headhunters are not accustomed to providing that kind of information, but directors shouldn't hesitate to ask. Further, directors should use their personal networks to learn as much as they can about the candidate.

Search committee members should insist on in-depth discussions with each outside candidate. The typical practice of meeting over dinner for an hour or two is grossly inadequate. The time is too short, and the venue is more conducive to polite social conversation than to the kind of intellectual probing that yields insight into the person's mind.

Directors too often touch superficially on the "soft" side of leadership, the hardest part of a CEO job. They ask questions that barely scratch the surface of leadership style, chemistry, and maturity. Nor do they spend enough time finding out what the candidate has actually accomplished and how. If something doesn't sound right, they keep quiet so as not to offend the person, particularly if the candidate is from a "good" company and is being pursued by others.

Questions should have enough rigor to give the search committee a good understanding of the candidate's strengths—and weaknesses. Everyone has them. For instance, if the candidate would be leading a large public company, find out how she or he feels about building a relationship with Wall Street. One newly hired CEO hated that part of the job, but no one knew that until after the appointment. Some shortcomings are easy to remedy. For instance, one board encouraged the CEO to hire a vice chairman to handle government relations because the CEO was weak in that area.

Allow time to get below the surface, by arranging to meet with the top three to four candidates over the course of a weekend, for instance. One or two directors should meet with each candidate for a minimum of two hours. After each interview, directors should share their views, compare notes, and design new questions. Once all the directors have spent time with each of the candidates and considered all the information, a consensus will begin to emerge. It is, in fact, uncanny how quickly judgments about people converge.

A Crucial Role for Boards

With the appointment of a successor comes a new challenge for the board: helping the new CEO achieve success quickly. A new CEO must take hold of the organization and the board early on and create momentum.

One way the board can help is through coaching. When a well-known high-tech company hired a new CEO in late 1999, the search committee ensured that two directors would be on call for coaching, mentoring, and use as a sounding board. In some cases, asking the retiring CEO to resign from the board helps the new leader take hold sooner.

Combining a rigorous selection process with well-honed instincts about people increases the odds of choosing the right person for the job. Helping the new CEO build momentum increases the chances that he or she will be successful in it.

Let there be no doubt that selection of a CEO is the most crucial job of a board. Directors must dedicate their time, energy, and passion to meeting this great and important leadership responsibility.

Ram Charan is coauthor of the landmark *Fortune* article "Why CEOs Fail" and an adviser on corporate governance, CEO succession, and strategy implementation. He was named as Best Teacher by Northwestern's Kellogg School and as a top-rated executive educator by *BusinessWeek*. He is author of *Boards at Work*, coauthor of *Every Business Is a Growth Business*, and a frequent contributor to *Harvard Business Review*.

Index

Leader to Leader

A quarterly publication of the Drucker Foundation and Jossey-Bass Publishers

Frances Hesselbein, Editor-in-Chief

Leader to Leader is a unique management publication, a quarterly report on management, leadership, and strategy written by today's top leaders *themselves*. Four times a year, Leader to Leader keeps you ahead of the curve by bringing you the latest offerings from a peerless selection of world-class executives, best-selling management authors, leading consultants, and respected social thinkers, making Leader to Leader unlike any other magazine or professional publication today.

Think of it as a short, intensive seminar with today's top thinkers and doers—people like Peter F. Drucker, Rosabeth Moss Kanter, Max De Pree, Charles Handy, Esther Dyson, Stephen Covey, Meg Wheatley, Peter Senge, and others.

Subscriptions to **Leader to Leader** are $199.00.
501(c)(3) nonprofit organizations can subscribe for $99.00 (must supply tax-exempt ID number when subscribing). Prices subject to change without notice.

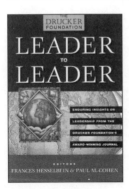

Leader to Leader

Enduring Insights on Leadership from the Drucker Foundation's Award-Winning Journal

Frances Hesselbein, Paul M. Cohen, Editors

The world's thought leaders come together in Leader to Leader, an inspiring examination of mission, leadership, values, innovation, building collaborations, shaping effective institutions, and creating community. Management pioneer Peter F. Drucker; Southwest Airlines CEO Herb Kelleher; best-selling authors Warren Bennis, Stephen R. Covey, and Charles Handy; Pulitzer Prize winner Doris Kearns Goodwin; Harvard professors Rosabeth Moss Kanter and Regina Herzlinger; and learning organization expert Peter Senge are among those who share their knowledge and experience in this essential resource. Their essays will spark ideas, open doors, and inspire all those who face the challenge of leading in an ever-changing environment.

For a reader's guide, see www.leaderbooks.org

Hardcover   ISBN 0-7879-4726-1 $27.00

FAX	CALL	MAIL	WEB
Toll Free	Toll Free	Jossey-Bass Publishers	Secure ordering at:
24 hours a day:	6am to 5pm PST:	989 Market St.	www.josseybass.com
800-605-2665	800-956-7739	San Francisco, CA 94105-1741	

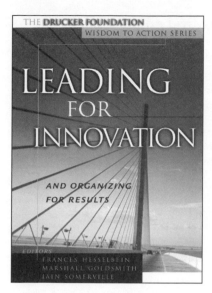

Leading for Innovation

And Organizing for Results

Frances Hesselbein,
Marshall Goldsmith,
and Iain Somerville

*From the Drucker Foundation's
Wisdom to Action Series*

**Renowned thought leaders
offer their insights on innovation**

Peter Drucker defines innovation as "change that creates a new dimension of performance." Leaders can create environments, give people the tools, and set the expectation to make innovation part of daily work. In this second volume of the Drucker Foundation's Wisdom to Action Series, twenty-seven remarkable thought leaders help today's leaders meet the challenge of releasing the power of innovation.

Leading for Innovation brings together Clayton M. Christensen, Jim Collins, Howard Gardner, Charles Handy, Rosabeth Moss Kanter, C. William Pollard, Margaret Wheatley, and other thought leaders to offer practical guidance for those who seek to lead their organizations to a new dimension of performance.

These thoughtful and incisive essays are essential resources for executives from the business, nonprofit, and government sectors as well as for consultants and board members.

Hardcover   ISBN 0-7879-5359-8 $27.95

FAX	CALL	MAIL	WEB
Toll Free	Toll Free	Jossey-Bass Publishers	Secure ordering at:
24 hours a day:	6am to 5pm PST:	989 Market St.	www.josseybass.com
800-605-2665	800-956-7739	San Francisco, CA 94105-1741	www.leaderbooks.com

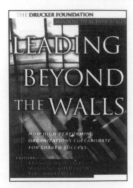

Leading Beyond the Walls

Frances Hesselbein, Marshall Goldsmith,
Iain Somerville, Editors

from the Drucker Foundation's Wisdom to Action Series

"There is need for acceptance on the part of leaders in every single institution, and in every single sector, that they, as leaders, have two responsibilities. They are responsible and accountable for the performance of their institution, and that has to be concentrated, focused, limited. They are responsible however, also, for the community as a whole. This requires commitment. It requires willingness to accept that other institutions have different values, respect for these values, and willingness to learn what these values are. It requires hard work. But above all, it requires commitment; conviction; dedication to the Common Good. Yes, each institution is autonomous and has to do its own work the way each instrument in an orchestra plays its own part. But there is also the 'score,' the community. And only if the individual instrument contributes to the score is there music. Otherwise there is only noise. This book is about the score."

—Peter F. Drucker

Increasingly, leaders and their organizations work in ways that extend beyond the walls of the enterprise. These partnerships, alliances, and networks allow organizations to achieve new levels of performance. At the same time, they create new challenges. Leaders "beyond the walls" must be adept at building and maintaining relationships, comfortable in working with individuals and organizations they cannot control, and able to move beyond the old preconceptions.

Leading Beyond the Walls presents insights from over twenty-five thought leaders from all three sectors, exploring the challenges and opportunities of partnership as well as the unique practices and perspectives that have helped individuals and organizations become more effective.

Paperback   ISBN 0-7879-5555-8 $16.50

FAX	CALL	MAIL	WEB
Toll Free	Toll Free	Jossey-Bass Publishers	Secure ordering at:
24 hours a day:	6am to 5pm PST:	989 Market St.	www.josseybass.com
800-605-2665	800-956-7739	San Francisco, CA 94105-1741	

The Drucker Foundation Future Series

All Three Volumes in a Slipcover Case

Boxed Set   ISBN 0-7879-4696-6 $80.00
Paperback Set ISBN 0-7879-5370-9 $49.00

Business Week Best-Seller!
The Leader of the Future
New Visions, Strategies, and Practices for the Next Era
Frances Hesselbein, Marshall Goldsmith, Richard Beckhard, Editors

World-class contributors offer insights into the future quality of our lives, businesses, organizations, society, and the leadership required to move us into the exciting unknown.

Hardcover   ISBN 0-7879-0180-6 $26.00
Paperback   ISBN 0-7879-0935-1 $18.00

Now in Paperback!
The Organization of the Future
Frances Hesselbein, Marshall Goldsmith, Richard Beckhard, Editors

"Required reading. If you don't use this book to help guide your organization through the changes, you may well be left behind."   —*Nonprofit World*

Hardcover   ISBN 0-7879-0303-5 $26.00
Paperback   ISBN 0-7879-5203-6 $18.00

Now in Paperback!
The Community of the Future
Frances Hesselbein, Marshall Goldsmith, Richard Beckhard, Richard F. Schubert, Editors

"This book of essays is full of rampant idealism. Its authors share a desire to better the world through their ideas and actions."   —*Christian Science Monitor*

Hardcover   ISBN 0-7879-1006-6 $26.00
Paperback   ISBN 0-7879-5204-4 $18.00

FAX	CALL	MAIL	WEB
Toll Free	Toll Free	Jossey-Bass Publishers	Secure ordering at:
24 hours a day:	6am to 5pm PST:	989 Market St.	www.josseybass.com
800-605-2665	800-956-7739	San Francisco, CA 94105-1741	

Leading in a Time of Change

A conversation between Peter F. Drucker and Peter M. Senge

Peter F. Drucker, Peter M. Senge, and Frances Hesselbein

Sit at the table with the visionary leaders who are setting the agenda for organizational leadership and change.

The Drucker Foundation presents a conversation with Peter F. Drucker and Peter M. Senge, hosted by Frances Hesselbein. In this dynamic package—which includes a video and companion workbook—two great minds of modern management share their wisdom on how leaders can prepare themselves and their organizations for the inevitable changes that lie ahead.

Watch the video and witness a remarkable conversation between Peter Drucker and Peter Senge as they talk about the importance of learning to lead change for all organizations. Using the principles presented in this stimulating video and workbook, you can help transform your organization into a change leader. In their discussion Drucker and Senge reveal how you can:

- Develop systematic methods to look for and anticipate change.

- Focus on and invest in opportunities rather than problems.

- Phase out established products and services.

- Balance change and continuity.

- Motivate and retain top performers and create a mind-set among employees that embraces positive change.

The companion workbook will be an invaluable aid in making strategic decisions. It will also serve as a fundamental resource for planning and implementing changes within your organization. This extraordinary package is an ideal tool for executive retreats, management training, and personal leadership development.

42-minute video with companion Viewer's Workbook ISBN 0-7879-5603-1 $195.00

FAX	CALL	MAIL	WEB
Toll Free	Toll Free	Jossey-Bass Publishers	Secure ordering at:
24 hours a day:	6am to 5pm PST:	989 Market St.	www.josseybass.com
800-605-2665	800-956-7739	San Francisco, CA 94105-1741